Praise for *The Power Presenter*

"Jerry is a coach like no other. If you need to give an important presentation, buy this book. Now. The only thing at stake is your income, your influence, and the success of your cause."

—*Scott Cook*
founder & chairman of the Executive Committee, Intuit, Inc.

"Jerry Weissman's genius is getting successful leaders like me to realize we are imbeciles when it comes to effective communication that is not email. In particular, Jerry broadens one's perspective on how to use the visual well, how to focus on the audience's perspective and on how to keep the narrative strong and compelling. I benefited from Jerry's work way back in 1995 for my first IPO, and then went back again in 2002 for my second IPO – in both cases his teaching added tremendous clarity to our investor presentations. Not only should IPO-bound CEOs read this book, but everyone who does presentations should absorb its messages."

—*Reed Hastings*
founder, chairman, and CEO, Netflix, Inc.

"If you've ever had butterflies when standing before an audience, this book is for you. Jerry Weissman is one of the world's experts in teaching people to overcome their nerves, and his secret starts with something very natural—the comfort we feel when having a conversation with one other person."

—*Chip Heath*
co-author, *Made to Stick: Why Some Ideas Survive and Others Die*

"This book will help you bring out your natural charisma. It's like a bottle of turbo-charged personality. Take a swig, and you'll kick butt."

—*Guy Kawasaki*
co-founder of Alltop.com, Author of *Reality Check*

"I watched with my own eyes as Jerry Weissman created billions in stock market value by teaching CEOs his speaking styles and strategies. Now it's all in a 250 page book—how cool is that?"

—*Andy Kessler*
Bestselling author of *Wall Street Meat and Running Money*

"As an executive communication coach, Jerry Weissman has taught me and many others that great communication skills are not hereditary, but can be learned. Jerry's series of books makes his profound ideas accessible to every reader. This book, *The Power Presenter*, is an excellent exposition into what makes a great communicator, and how to become one, starting from the inside. Using the very persuasion techniques it teaches, this book applies plain language, fun examples, and convincing demonstrations to lead the reader to absorb and internalize the concepts, and gain the skills and confidence to truly become a power presenter."

—*Kai-fu Lee*
vice president, Google Inc.; president, Greater China

"*The Power Presenter* captures the essence of Jerry's in-person training, including his approach, real world examples and story-telling strategies. It's a must read for anyone who needs to close a deal, market a product or drive consensus."

—*Mike Nash*
corporate vice president, Windows Product Management,
Microsoft Corporation

"Jerry's insightful coaching helped us to launch a major new chip design successfully. His new book, *The Power Presenter*, makes the invaluable techniques he showed us at Intel available to everyone."

—*David Perlmutter*
executive vice president; general manager, Mobility
Group, Intel Corporation

"Jerry has the uncanny ability to take the art of communicating and make it feel like science-*The Power Presenter* is a prescriptive roadmap to communications confidence and excellence."

—*Ron Ricci*
vice president, Corporate Positioning, Cisco Systems

"Customers determine business success, audiences determine presentation success. Capture your audiences with *The Power Presenter*."

—*Patricia Seybold*
author of *Outside Innovation*, *The Customer Revolution*, and
Customers.com

THE
POWER
PRESENTER

THE
POWER
PRESENTER

Technique, Style, and Strategy from America's Top Speaking Coach

---

JERRY WEISSMAN

John Wiley & Sons, Inc.

Published by John Wiley & Sons, Inc., Hoboken, New Jersey
Published simultaneously in Canada

For general information on our other products and services or for technical support, please contact our Customer Care Department within the United States at (800) 762-2974, outside the United States at (317) 572-3993 or fax (317) 572-4002.

Wiley also publishes its books in a variety of electronic formats. Some content that appears in print may not be available in electronic books. For more information about Wiley products, visit our web site at www.wiley.com.

Library of Congress Cataloging-in-Publication Data:

Weissman, Jerry.
   The power presenter : technique, style, and strategy from America's top speaking coach/Jerry Weissman.
      p. cm.
   Includes index.
   ISBN 978-0-470-37648-5 (cloth)
   1. Public speaking. I. Title.
   PN4129.15.W45 2009
   808.5′1—dc22

                                                                                2008032244

Printed in the United States of America.

10 9 8 7 6 5

For Benji Rosen
A launch from Houston to the moon—and the stars

CONTENTS

The Wrong Way and the Right Way to Coach Presentations

Dizzy Gillespie, the legendary jazz trumpet player, known as the father of bebop, was once asked how he created the distinctive musical form. He described one particular performance during which, after a rather indulgent night, he improvised a new elliptical, free-form sound. Nonetheless, his fellow musicians heralded the resultant effort as a creative breakthrough and started emulating his style. Dizzy shook his head and observed, "Man, them cats was just copying my mistakes!"

In a reverse route, at the beginning of my career as a speaking coach, I spent many tortuous, torturous, and torturing hours copying the mistakes of conventional presentation skills training, treating businesspeople as performers, thus perpetuating a counterproductive approach for both the instructed and the instructor. The very word *training* denotes rigorous discipline; while *coaching*, derived from the word for a transportation vehicle, denotes movement. My goal was to move the businesspeople I coached to become successful presenters *naturally*.

In search of solutions to my dilemma, I looked back on my days as a producer of public affairs programs at WCBS-TV in New York City. A key part of my job was to invite men and women from the government, academic, health, scientific, and culture sectors—none of them performers—into our studios. To help make these people feel comfortable and look comfortable in the stressful circumstance of appearing on camera, we leveraged the basic format of public affairs television: the talk show. By structuring our programs as conversations—person-to-person interviews or small group discussions conducted by professional moderators—we put our nonprofessional guests into familiar settings that promptly reduced their stress levels.

Another part of my job was to screen hours and hours of new and archival film and videotape, conduct hours and hours of interviews, read stacks and stacks of reports, and condense all of that information into a clear 28-minute-and-40-second program. In doing so, I developed an array of techniques to distill and focus ideas.

Looking at those two job functions in retrospect made me realize that control of content and control of mind would make the stressful circumstances of speaking in public or delivering presentations less onerous for business people—and for all human beings for whom standing in front of an audience provokes a fear equal to, if not greater than, that of heights, insects, or flying.

At that moment, the vicious cycle of copying mistakes ended and the Mental Method of Presenting began. I started my own coaching business, Power Presentations, and developed a broad set of techniques to help presenters and speakers clear their minds by organizing their stories, then to deliver them as a series of conversations rather than as performances.

Déjà vu! Businesspeople in Silicon Valley promptly experienced the same comfort in presentations as did our guests in the CBS studios. Now that this powerful methodology has evolved and proven successful for two decades, allow me introduce its techniques to you so that you can learn how to feel natural and appear confident whenever you stand in front of *any* audience.

How Speaking Style and Delivery Can Raise the Value of an IPO

The Universal Challenge

Cisco originally expected to get $13.50 to $15.50 per share for its stock. "But during the road show the company was so well-received" that it managed to sell 2.8 million shares at $18 apiece, Valentine [chairman of the Board of Cisco Systems] said. He attributed "at least $2 to $3" of the increase to Weissman's coaching.

—San Francisco Chronicle, July 9, 1990[1]

When a business offers shares of its stock to the public for the first time, the company's senior management team develops a presentation that they take on the road to potential investors. They visit about a dozen cities across the country (and often across the ocean, as well) over a two-week period, delivering the same pitch several times a day, or about 30 or 40 times each week. It's the most demanding and high-stakes presentation any executive will ever make. That's why they bring me in to coach them.

Why should you care about a nearly twenty-year-old article about Cisco Systems' road show? What does the initial public offering (IPO) of one of the most successful companies in the world mean to you? And what does a powerful endorsement of my presentation coaching mean to you?

After all, since only a few hundred companies go public in any given year, you are more likely to win a national lottery than to launch an IPO. But you'll almost certainly have to give a presentation or to make an important speech at some point during your lifetime. And whether you are a businessman or businesswoman or an ordinary citizen, your challenge is to be as "well-received" as the Cisco Systems IPO road show.

The same technique, style, and strategy that I provided to the Cisco executive team and, subsequently, to the executive teams of more than 500 other companies preparing for their IPO road shows (among them, Intuit, Netflix, Dolby Labs, and Yahoo!) can help *you* with every presentation or speech you will ever have to deliver. My presentation techniques have also helped thousands of executives, salespeople, and engineers at Microsoft, Intel, and an additional 500 other companies to sell products, propose partnerships, raise financing, or seek approval for projects. This book provides you with the same techniques that executives pay thousands of dollars to learn in my private coaching sessions.

As important as delivery style is in business presentations it is of equal importance when soliciting funds for a not-for-profit cause, or addressing the assemblage of a professional association, community organization, church, or synagogue. In all cases, whenever and wherever you have to stand and deliver, your challenge is to make your presentation or speech a success.

John Morgridge, the CEO who delivered the Cisco Systems IPO road show was faced with such a challenge in 1990. At the time, John was an experienced executive. As a businessman, however, John was focused more on delivering his data than on his presentation style and technique. His challenge was further compounded by the fact that Cisco's innovative networking technology was complex, which made the company's IPO story difficult to understand by nontechnical audiences of institutional fund managers.

In our work together, I coached John to craft a story that was comprehensible and meaningful to potential investors, and to deliver it to them with poise, confidence, and enthusiasm. Through it all, I helped John to feel and appear comfortable, despite the natural apprehension that all human beings experience when speaking in public about important issues. History is witness to John's success. Cisco's Chairman of the Board, Don Valentine, estimated that my presentation coaching added millions of dollars in value to the company's IPO. John went on to build Cisco into a formidable business enterprise, and now, having retired, he is building a formidable philanthropic enterprise.

Sixteen years later, and more than 500 other IPO client companies after the Cisco IPO, Steve Goldman, the CEO of Isilon Systems, retained my services for his road show. Isilon, a Seattle company that makes clustered storage systems and software for digital content, had a technical story to tell. "Coaching helped us to elevate our message," Steve told *Business 2.0 Magazine*. And elevate it did: on the first day of trading, Isilon shares jumped 77 percent, the best launch of a technology IPO in more than six years. Steve called this, "Ka-ching!"[2]

Another CEO experienced a similar challenge during his IPO, but with a different twist. Just as his road show was about to begin, the CEO learned that there was a problem back at the home office. To deal with the problem, he frequently had to get on the telephone between presentations. As a result, whenever he presented during that first week, he was distracted. Not surprisingly, his presentations suffered.

Over the intervening weekend, the CEO finally cleared up the problem. No longer distracted, he presented smoothly during the entire second week. At the end of the road show, the investment bankers tallied the results of their efforts. The cities they visited during the first week had placed light orders, and the cities of the second week high orders. The pivotal point here is that the content of the presentation was identical during both weeks; the only difference was the CEO's body language and voice. Speaking style and delivery can indeed raise the value of an IPO.

The most recent addition to the IPO marketplace is http://retail roadshow.com, a Web site where anyone with a browser can, after clicking on a Preliminary Prospectus disclaimer, view a road show. The presentation is then seen as a split screen: on one side is a video recording of the executive officers of a company delivering their pitch; on the other is their slide show, advancing in synchronization with their narrative.

Despite this new, unrestricted access, the investment bankers running these offerings still arrange the usual two-week tour for the company's management team, during which they visit those dozen cities and deliver those 30 or 40 iterations of their road show each of those weeks, just as they did before RetailRoadshow came into being in 2005. The reason for this grueling tour is that no investor will make a decision to buy millions of dollars of stock (as are most such IPO orders) based on a canned presentation alone. Investors want to meet the executives in person, press the flesh, look them in the eye, and interact with them directly.

The challenge then is to make that vital interaction a success. John Morgridge of Cisco faced that challenge, as do all the CEOs of all

IPO road shows, as does every man or woman who delivers *any* presentation or speech; a universal challenge heightened by the all-too-human reaction to the all-too-familiar pressure of standing in front of a live audience.

The Deer in the Headlights

Picture this: You're seated in the audience for a speech or a presentation. At the start, the speaker approaches the front of the room, reaches the lectern, turns to face the group, and suddenly freezes, striking the pose of the proverbial deer in the headlights. The eyes widen like dinner plates. The body goes rigid. Then, as the person starts to speak, the parched lips emit a thin, rasping sound, and the halting words that sputter out are punctuated by a series of audible pasty clicks. In response to the cotton mouth, the person's arm darts down to the lectern to grasp a glass of water and, as the trembling hand lifts the glass, the water almost sloshes over the edge.

Why does this happen? Why would speaking, a most ordinary activity that most people practice every day with complete ease, become so fraught with dread when it takes place in front of an audience? Why wouldn't every man or woman who stands to deliver a presentation or a speech be energized about the challenge? After all, many presentations or speeches are mission-critical situations, where a favorable outcome hangs in the balance of the success or failure of the message and the messenger.

There's the rub: the mission-critical situation, the Moment of Truth. At the very instant the presentation begins, when the audience sits back and falls silent, and the presenter or speaker becomes the focal point of attention, he or she suddenly thinks, "Uh-oh! They're all looking at me!" "I'm on the spot!" "I'd better do well!"

Fight-or-Flight

Speaking before a group is widely considered to be one of the most anxiety-ridden experiences known to humankind. That is because it triggers a physiological response equal to that of all other known fears: a surge of adrenaline that produces the classic Fight-or-Flight Syndrome. Adrenaline is the *cause;* Fight-or-Flight is the *effect,* and the result is either defensive or anxious behavior. This involuntary physical reaction impacts all God's creatures, all human beings, including *every* person who presents, veteran and novice alike—even professional performers. The great British actor Sir Laurence Olivier, classical pianists Glenn Gould and Sviatoslav Richter, and popular singers Barbra Streisand and Carly Simon, have all acknowledged that they suffer from stage fright, the performers' version of the fear of public speaking.[3] The common culprit in all these cases is the adrenaline rush. Imagine that: *The very system that enables an organism to survive in the wild causes it to falter or fail in the captive environment of a presentation or speech.*

Reducing the Adrenaline Rush

Recommendations for remedies to stem the adrenaline rush abound. If you do an Internet search on the fear of public speaking, you'll find *millions* of entries, among them:

- Take deep breaths.
- Do push-ups.
- Run around the block.
- Perform yoga.
- Make a fist.
- Yawn.
- Focus on an imaginary spot in the back of the room.
- Pop a pill (beta-blockers are the drug of choice).
- Take a swig of alcohol.

- Imagine your audience naked.
- Have sex.

The list goes on, but its length and variety bear testament that the problem remains unsolved. That is because most of them are purely physical solutions to what is *not* a purely physical problem. Moreover, a physical approach to overcoming the fear of public speaking will make a presenter or speaker feel like a performer, and exacerbate the problem that caused the adrenaline to start pumping in the first place.

The adrenaline rush is caused by the presenter or speaker's *mental* perception that danger is imminent. So, unless that perception is dealt with at the outset, the adrenaline will continue its detrimental rampage unabated.

The Mental Method of Presenting

The key is to attack the problem at the Moment of Truth: when the presentation begins. Attack the problem at the instant your audience settles back, falls silent, all eyes turn to look at you—and you clutch. It is precisely at that very instant when you can exert the power of your mind to control the forces of your body.

The Mental Method of Presenting is *a psychological solution for a physiological problem*. It is a step-by-step process that will enable you to exert that control. I have battle-tested this method for two decades, coaching thousands of clients to present with composure and assurance.

The following pages will show you how to implement the Mental Method of Presenting and, in so doing, overcome your fear of public speaking, reduce your adrenaline rush, and with it, the negative effects of Fight or Flight. The Mental Method will enable you to put into action the time-honored adage: "*If you have butterflies, make them fly in formation.*"

You'll learn how to optimize those equally important physical factors: your eyes, your body language, your voice, and—the subject of the most frequently asked question about presentation skills—what to do with your hands and arms. You'll also learn how to integrate the design and animation of your slides with your narrative and delivery skills in an exclusive technique called Graphics Synchronization. Along the way, you'll progress through the essential stages of the learning process and, with it, discover how to break old habits and develop a new confidence in your ability to speak effectively and comfortably in public.

As a presentations coach, I have a special fascination with the delivery styles of political figures. Throughout this book you'll find many historic examples of notable speakers whose techniques affected the outcome of elections, if not changed the world. In the 2008 U.S. presidential election, Barack Obama's oratorical talent was, by any measure, a major feature during the entire campaign. It was a driving factor in his come-from-behind victory over his opponent for the Democratic nomination, Hillary Rodham Clinton and, ultimately, his triumph over his Republican opponent, John McCain. We'll look in detail at the techniques of Barack Obama's delivery style in chapter 10—techniques that you can use in your own presentations and speeches.

You'll also discover what to do and what not to do from detailed analyses of other famous politicians and public figures, among them Ronald Reagan, Bill Clinton, Martin Luther King, and John F. Kennedy. These examples are drawn from an extensive collection of archival film and video tapes that I've edited and narrated to support and illustrate the main points in the book. The live sequences with commentary are available on our Web site: www.powerltd.com/video_access.htm.

We've captured the key moment in each of the clips, referred to throughout the book as "video frames," and inserted them into the text as still pictures, along with other photographs and graphic illustrations. Please study these images, view the videos, learn the techniques, practice them diligently and *you* will become a Power Presenter.

Your Actions Speak Louder than Your Words

Speak (verb) 5a. To convey a message by nonverbal means: Actions speak louder than words.
> —*The American Heritage Dictionary of the English Language*
> Fourth Edition, 2000

Audience Advocacy

One of the most important concepts I teach my private clients is Audience Advocacy, a viewpoint that asks you, the presenter, to become an advocate for your audience. Put yourself into your audience's place and think about their hopes, fears, and passions. Consider what your audience knows about you and your message or cause, and what they need to know in order to respond favorably to you, to act on your call to action.

All these factors are a measure of how your audience responds to you intellectually. Yet Audience Advocacy applies equally to how your audience responds to you interpersonally; to the physical delivery of your story via your body language and your voice. In this view, your audience's perception of you then widens from their minds to include their eyes and their ears, and even more deeply, their guts. How do they *feel* about you?

Think of the presenter and the audience as the beginning and ending points of *all* interpersonal communications; then think of the presenter as a transmitter and the audience as a receiver. The presenter transmits a set of dynamics—human dynamics—that can be summed up in three Vs:

- *Verbal.* The story you tell.
- *Vocal.* Your voice, or how *you* tell your story.
- *Visual.* The third dynamic refers not to your Microsoft PowerPoint slides, but to *you*, your body language, and *what* you do when you tell your story.

Your audiences are affected by these three dynamics to varying degrees. Their relative impact is seen in the pie chart in Figure 1.1.

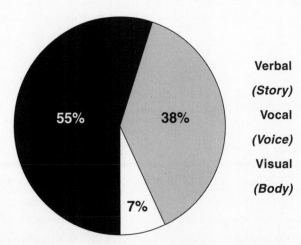

Figure 1.1   The Relative Impact of Human Dynamics Query

The largest wedge is in black at 55 percent; moving clockwise, the middle one in gray is at 38 percent, and the smallest wedge is in white at 7 percent. You'll note that the labels are not connected to the wedges. How do you think they rank? Which has the greatest impact? Which has the least? We've left the rest of this page blank for you to think about the question. You'll find the answer on the next page in Figure 1.2.

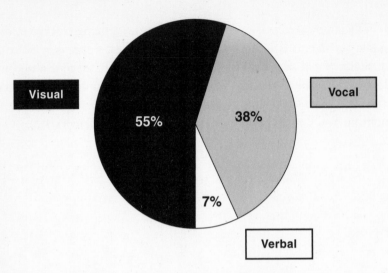

Figure 1.2   The Relative Impact of Human Dynamics

The largest wedge is the Visual at 55 percent; moving clockwise, the middle wedge, the Vocal, is 38 percent, and the smallest, the Verbal, is 7 percent. The body language has the greatest impact, the voice, next, while the story has the least impact.*

---

*These dynamics are my variation of a widely known 1981 study called "Silent Messages," conducted by Professor Albert Mehrabian of the Department of Psychology at the University of California, Los Angeles. The findings in "Silent Messages" were: "Total liking = 7% verbal liking + 38% vocal liking + 55% facial liking." Professor Mehrabian also specifically limited his findings to "apply only when a person is communicating about emotions and definitely do not apply to communication in general."[1]

I have extended "facial liking" to include the entire array of Visual aspects: the eyes, features, head, hands, arms, and posture. I have also widened my view to how these factors impact *all* forms of human communication, ranging from person-to-person conversation all the way through to our primary focus; presentations, and speeches. Furthermore, I intend to demonstrate that all of these human encounters do indeed involve emotion. In fact, as you'll discover in the next chapter, emotion is present in *all* interpersonal communication *involuntarily*; a powerful dynamic proven by other scientific studies made more than a decade after Professor Mehrabian's work.

Impact

Surprised? You're not alone. For the past 20 years, I've been showing this pie chart—without the labels—to my private clients and asking them the same question I just asked you. Although I haven't kept a formal tally, I can safely tell you that the large majority of them were also surprised by the answer.

Given the amount of time and effort that most presenters and speakers expend scribbling on yellow legal pads, pounding away at their computers, or shuffling their slides in preparation for their mission-critical presentations, they assume that content is paramount; but at the Moment of Truth, the story takes third place behind the body language and the voice.

There is ample support for these dynamics, starting with the examples of the impact of delivery skills in the IPO and political arenas you read about in the introduction, and continuing with a string of further evidence from other arenas in the balance of this chapter.

Consider Ronald Reagan, known as the "Great Communicator," and deservedly so for his peerless skills as a public speaker. No president in history of the United States achieved the level of popularity ratings that Reagan did. During his eight years in office (1981 to 1989) he brought personality to the forefront of presidential qualities. In an office that previously had been occupied by professional politicians, former generals, or career bureaucrats. Reagan's persona radiated a subtle but irresistible charisma that held the national news media, the electorate—and every audience he ever faced—in his thrall.

The measure of Reagan's impact was best expressed in a reaction to what was to be his presidential swan song: a pass-the-baton speech in support of his imminent replacement, then-Vice President George

H.W. Bush. On August 15, 1988, at the Republican National Convention in New Orleans, the assembled delegates in the enormous Louisiana Superdome, and the even more enormous prime-time television audience, watched enchanted as Reagan poured on the charm.

With George Bush, I'll know as we approach the new millennium our children will have a future secure with a nation at peace and protected against aggression. We'll have a prosperity that spreads to the blessings of our abundance and opportunity that spreads across all America. We'll have safe and active neighborhoods, drug-free schools that send our children soaring in the atmosphere of great ideas and deep values. And a nation, confidently willing to take its leadership into the uncharted reaches of a new age. So George, I'm in your corner. I'm ready to volunteer . . .

The partisan crowd in the Superdome interrupted, rising to their feet to roar their approval and flourish their blue and white "Bush '88" banners in a tidal wave of affection. Reagan smiled humbly and, then, with exquisite graciousness, continued:

. . . I'm ready to volunteer a little advice now and then, offer a pointer or two on strategy. If asked. I'll help keep the facts straight or just stand back and cheer; but, George, just one personal request . . .

At this point Reagan paused for dramatic effect, his eyes crinkling and his lips pursing. Then his lips parted into that classic sunny smile (Video Frame 1.1).

Video Frame 1.1   Ronald Reagan Endorses George H.W. Bush

Note

To see this live video clip from Ronald Reagan's speech with commentary, please visit www.powerltd.com/tpp and use the pass code you saw in the introduction.

Now Reagan resumed delivering the big payoff to his speech with his trademark signature phrase:

Go out there and win one for the Gipper![2]

Among the viewers of the nationwide telecast was the Pulitzer Prize-winning television critic of the *Los Angeles Times*, Howard Rosenberg, who summed up his reaction in his column the next day.

There is a critical moment early in every Reagan speech when his physical presence begins to eclipse his words—when you begin watching more and hearing less—feeling more and thinking less. Look and mood completely take over. That presence on TV: just the sight of him cocking his head with his sincere grin and lopsided hair, is still worth a thousand words and millions of votes.[3]

The Visual dominated the Vocal and the Verbal.

An equally powerful, but *converse* example of Howard Rosenberg's reaction to Ronald Reagan comes from Oliver Sacks, a prominent physician (professor of Clinical Neurology and Clinical Psychiatry at the Columbia University College of Physicians and Surgeons), and also a prominent author. In his bestselling book, *The Man Who Mistook His Wife for a Hat and Other Clinical Tales*, Dr. Sacks described his work with *aphasic* (brain-damaged) patients. In one incident, Dr. Sacks entered a ward to find most of the patients there watching President Reagan deliver a speech on television and *laughing at him hysterically*.

Dr. Sacks explained:

Why all this? Because speech—natural speech—does not consist of words alone. . . . It consists of utterance—an uttering-forth of one's whole meaning with one's whole being—the understanding of which involves infinitely more than mere word recognition. And this was the clue to aphasics' understanding, even when they might be wholly uncomprehending of words as such. For though the words, the verbal constructions, per se, might convey nothing, spoken language is normally suffused with "tone," embedded in an expressiveness which transcends the verbal.[4]

The Visual dominates the Vocal and the Verbal.

As further evidence of these dynamics, let's turn back to September 23, 1960, a day at the height of the Cold War. Soviet Premier Nikita Khrushchev, the contentious leader of the Communist bloc, had come to New York to attend a session of the United Nations General Assembly. During a speech by the British Prime Minister Khrushchev, who was seated in the audience, angrily pounded his fists on the desk, disrupting the session. When he stepped up to the green marble podium to deliver his own speech, Khrushchev unleashed a vehement attack against the West, the United Nations, and particularly, against the United States.

Most of the delegates in that international audience had only Khrushchev's body language, the 55 percent to react to. They certainly did not understand his Russian, the 7 percent nor did they have his own voice, the 38 percent, as they heard only an interpreter's translation of his words via headphones. But Khrushchev's powerfully expressive gestures left no doubt whatsoever about his message (Video Frame 1.2).

Video Frame 1.2 Soviet Premier Nikita Khrushchev at the United Nations

> **Note**
>
> To see this live video clip from Nikita Khrushchev's speech with commentary, please visit www.powerltd.com/tpp and use the pass code you saw in the introduction.

Khrushchev's dramatic presentation was so memorable that when, 46 years later, during another session of the United Nations General Assembly, Hugo Chavez, the contentious president of Venezuela, stood at that same green marble podium and delivered a fiery attack on the United States, the *New York Times* called it "A Speech That Khrushchev or Arafat or Che Would Admire."[5]

As memorable was Khrushchev's 1960 speech in New York, an even more memorable rhetorical event took place just three days later in Chicago: Richard M. Nixon and John F. Kennedy, respectively the Republican and Democratic candidates for president, met in the first-ever televised election debate. Nixon, the favorite, appeared nervous and rigid, while Kennedy, the underdog, appeared confident and poised. The day after the debate, their positions in the public opinion polls reversed. You'll see this encounter analyzed in detail in chapter 7, but, taken together, both events vividly demonstrate how the *Visual dynamics dominate both the Vocal and Verbal; or, why actions speak louder than words*.

Actions Speak Louder Than Words

Actions are the Visual, the 55 percent; *speak* is the Vocal, the 38 percent; and *words* are the Verbal, the 7 percent.

For the purest example of these dynamics, let's turn to a form of communication in which *only* the Visual element exists: pantomime. This ancient art, which had its origins in classical Greek and Roman drama and its development in sixteenth-century Italian *commedia dell'arte*, does not involve either the Vocal or the Verbal dynamic. In mime, the body language alone tells the entire story silently and accounts for 100 percent of the impact.

The most famous example of this art is seen in the work of one of the world's greatest mimes, Marcel Marceau. For decades, Marceau captivated audiences around the globe with his wordless performances. One in particular was his portrayal of the ages of man in a piece called "Birth, Youth, Maturity, Old Age, and Death." Mr. Marceau began the sequence curled up in the fetal position and then, slowly, in one unbroken sequence, opened up and became a toddling infant. Continuing fluidly, he stretched his limbs and the infant transformed into a strapping young man, striding vigorously ahead in place. But soon his strides slowed down, his shoulders hunched over, and he became an old man, doddering forward until he concluded in a shriveled ball, a mirror image of the fetal position at the start. (Photograph 1.1)

Photograph 1.1　Marcel Marceau

"One critic said, 'He accomplishes in less than two minutes what most novelists cannot do in volumes.' "[6]

> **Note**
>
> To see a video of another mime, please visit www.powerltd.com/ tpp and use the pass code you saw in the introduction.

Actions speak louder than words. The Visual dominates the Vocal and the Verbal.

To bring these dynamics from the stage to the real world, try this simple exercise: Ask a colleague or friend to be your audience for a very brief presentation. Then step up to the front of the room and start to speak, but do so silently, moving your lips without using your voice. As you do, slouch, put your weight on one foot, thrust your hands deep into your pockets, and dart your eyes rapidly around the room. Next, suddenly, while continuing to move your lips silently, stand up straight, look directly at your colleague, address all of your energies to him or her, and extend your hand toward that person, as if you were about to shake hands.

Then stop the exercise and ask your trial audience member to react. Undoubtedly, the person will respond negatively to the first part of your exercise and positively to the second. The response will be solely to your Visual dynamics.

For scientific validation of this phenomenon, we turn to David McNeill, professor emeritus, Departments of Psychology and Linguistics at the University of Chicago, who conducted studies in a subject he called, "communicative effects of speech-mismatched gestures." The subjects in the study were shown a videotape in which speakers told a story, but with gestures that differed oddly from the content. After the story, the subjects were asked to retell the story from memory. The subjects described what they *saw*, rather than what they *heard*. They described the gestures, not the words.[7]

The irony is that most presenters and speakers spend most of their time and effort on the Verbal content. Therefore, am I suggesting that you should forget about the art of telling your story and focus on your delivery skills? Not at all. Put equal emphasis on *both* sides of the equation, as much on your body language and your voice as on your story; as much on the messenger as on the message.

Think of the elements of the equation as a delivery system and a payload. NASA expends millions of dollars and thousands of hours building a communications satellite. If the satellite is launched by a rocket that does not have sufficient boost, the satellite does not go into orbit. Your company or organization expends many dollars and countless hours preparing to launch a product, a service, or a campaign for a cause. That is the priceless payload. *You* are the delivery system. The *style* of your presentation must support the priceless *substance* of *your* message.

Launch your payload into orbit.

The Crucial Task: Creating Audience Empathy

We are wired to connect. Neuroscience has discovered that our brain's very design makes it sociable, inexorably drawn into an intimate brain-to-brain linkup whenever we engage with another person. That neural bridge lets us affect the brain—and so the body—of everyone we interact with, just as they do us.

—Daniel Goleman
Social Intelligence: The New Science of Human Relationships [1]

In addition to the Visual, Vocal, and Verbal forces that influence your audience, they are also impacted by another dynamic: *empathy*. Evolved from the Greek word for emotion or affection, empathy refers to shared or vicarious feelings—as distinct from *sympathy*, which is more about pity, and implies separate, rather than mutual feelings. In the presentation environment, the empathy is the shared feelings between the audience and the presenter, but the sharing on the audience's part is *involuntary*.

Empathy

To illustrate, let's revisit the deer in the headlights example from the introduction. As you sat in the audience for a speech or presentation, you saw a presenter step up to the lectern and suddenly freeze: the eyes widened, the body went rigid, the mouth got pasty, and the hand trembled. How did that make you feel? Most likely, you winced. You felt rather sorry for the presenter, if not even somewhat nervous yourself. In that one instant, your reaction was completely *visceral*.

Another common wince-inducing presentation situation is when a presenter steps into the bright beam of a high-intensity projector and suddenly squints in the light. Undoubtedly, you squint too.

That is empathy, a direct correlation between what the presenter *does* (Visual dynamics) and *says* (Vocal dynamics) and how the audience feels about the presenter; a link between the *presenter behavior* and the *audience perception* of the presenter.

While these separate dynamics are seemingly unrelated, there is an actual physiological link between the two. In 2004, a team of British researchers conducted a study measuring brain waves in empathic situations. In the experiment, volunteer couples were invited into a neurology laboratory where the scientists attached electrodes to each person's brain. First, one member of the couple received a mild electric shock, which produced an impulse in a particular area of that person's brain. Then the mild electric shock was administered to the second member of the couple. When the first person observed the partner's reaction to the shock, the same area of the first person's brain produced the same impulse as when he or she was shocked—even though that person was no longer experiencing the shock. What the first person *saw* produced the same reaction as he or she *felt*.

As the study summed it up:

Our ability to have an experience of another's pain is characteristic of empathy. Using functional imaging, we assessed brain activity while volunteers experienced a painful stimulus and compared it to that elicited when they observed a signal indicating that their loved one—present in the same room—was receiving a similar pain stimulus.[2]

Although you may not be the loved one of the stressed deer in the headlights presenter, when you are in the audience—present in the same room—and *see* that person's nervousness, you are most likely to *feel* similar, vicarious feelings. That is the power of empathy.

These vicarious feelings are due to *mirror neurons*, a set of nerve cells in the brain, which were first studied in 1992 by a team of Italian researchers working with laboratory monkeys. The study was intended to measure the animals' brain activity, but the scientists noted that the monkeys' physical behavior mimicked their own, leading the scientists to conclude:

These findings indicate that premotor neurons can retrieve movements not only on the basis of stimulus characteristics, as previously described, but also on the basis of the meaning of the observed actions.[3]

The article was circulated widely among other scientists who dubbed the mirror neurons, "monkey see, monkey do." In other words, what is *seen* is the same as what is *felt*.

The evolutionary path from monkeys to humans was apparent in a 2005 television documentary about mirror neurons on *Nova*, the PBS science series. While the program presented all the usual serious scientific evidence, including the preceding British and Italian experiments, the most illustrative—and entertaining—part of the program came when the series host and executive editor, Robert Krulwich, piled a stack of heavy boxes on top of one another and then carried them out into a street in New York City.

The stack was too high and very unstable, so Krulwich struggled and strained as he walked. As he passed other pedestrians, who were carrying nothing bulkier than purses or briefcases they, too, appeared strained. What they *saw* produced the same reaction as Krulwich *felt*.

The power of empathy works both ways. Different behavior by the presenter produces a different perception from the audience. Please recall the exercise in chapter 1 in which you gave two different versions of a brief presentation silently and asked your trial audience to respond only to your Visual dynamics. Recall, too, the deer in the headlights example we've been referencing. Imagine if that presenter had behaved differently—had stood up confidently, strode to the lectern briskly, smiled broadly, with both arms open wide in welcome, and then, with a steady hand, lifted the glass of water to take a sip—you, seated in the audience would surely have reacted positively. Instead of the vicarious nervousness you felt during the first version, you would be fully receptive to that person. And all of this occurs *before* the presenter or speaker utters a single word! Positive or negative, either way, *the audience responds to the presenter's behavior* **involuntarily**.

Then, when the presenter speaks and adds the Verbal component to the Visual and the Vocal, all the dynamics compound. Gathering momentum, the empathy begins to affect the audience's perception of the presenter's *story*. If the presenter appears poised and confident, the audience will perceive the content favorably; if the presenter exhibits anxiety, the audience will perceive the message dubiously or, worse, negatively.

Presenter Behavior/Audience Perception

For a case in point, let's flash back to May 15, 1996. Bob Dole, the veteran Senate majority leader decided to seek the Republican

Party candidacy to run against the incumbent, President Bill Clinton. Dole kicked off his campaign with a carefully choreographed speech to announce his resignation from the Senate (Video Frame 2.1).

Video Frame 2.1   Bob Dole Announces His Candidacy

Note

To see this live video clip from Bob Dole's speech with commentary, please visit www.powerltd.com/tpp and use the pass code you saw in the introduction.

With his adoring wife, Libby, at his side, and flanked by his longtime congressional colleagues, Dole concluded his launch speech with these words:

I am highly privileged to be my party's nominee and I am content that my faith and my story are for the American people to decide. But the American people have always known through our long and trying history that God has blessed the hard way. And because of this, as I say thank you and farewell to the Senate, as summer nears and as the campaign begins, my heart is buoyant . . .

When Bob Dole said, "My heart is buoyant," he said it flatly, his voice descending, making him sound anything but buoyant.

Then he concluded:

Thank you and may God guide us to what is right. Thank you very much.[4]

Libby hugged him warmly and his supporters applauded him politely, but the die was cast. Plain-spoken Bob Dole came out of the starting gate at a slow trot, forced to try and catch up to a charismatic Bill Clinton, who was already galloping at full speed. Dole was left at the post.

In this case we have a slight variation on the theme. The reserved body language and prosaic voice belonged to Bob Dole, but the Verbal content did not. The evocative words Dole spoke were written by Mark Helprin, a professional writer, who, in addition to being a respected political columnist, is also a successful and very talented novelist.

"As summer nears and as the campaign begins, my heart is buoyant," are a novelist's words, lyrical not prosaic. The delivery vehicle failed to lift the payload into orbit.

The mismatch—and the audience perception from the electorate—came in the 1996 public opinion polls conducted by CNN/USA *Today*/Gallup, shown in Figure 2.1. On the day Dole made his kickoff speech, he trailed Clinton, and he stayed behind him right through Election

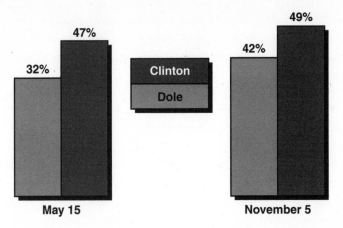

Figure 2.1   1996 Presidential Election: Starting Polls and Final Vote[5]

Day. The only reason Dole gained 10 points in the interval was that he no longer had opposition for the Republican candidacy.

Dry-as-dust Bob Dole was no match for the Bill Clinton charm. After the election, however, Dole realized how he might have competed more effectively: He adjusted his Verbal content to meet his own natural Vocal and Visual behavior. In a television commercial for a credit card company, he played his own homespun self and the ad became an instant media hit.

While Bob Dole didn't defeat Clinton, he did find his métier. In contrast, former California governor Gray Davis never stood a chance. The 2003 recall election for that state's governorship provides another example of the negative effect of negative behavior.

As the sitting governor, Gray Davis, had presided over a deep slide in the state's economy resulting in a massive budget deficit. His political opponents, seizing the opportunity, mounted a campaign to unseat him. In a land rush, 135 candidates registered to run in a recall election to replace Davis, but the clear favorite was the popular, macho Hollywood movie star, Arnold Schwarzenegger. It was no contest.

The actor coasted to victory by a wide margin. While California's budget and economy were major factors, a key differential was Davis's dour persona which paled by comparison with Schwarzenegger's dazzle.

Neither you nor any presenter or speaker could, or should, expect to compete with a professional actor or performer. Any effort to do so would produce disastrous results. Businesspeople are hired for their jobs on the basis of their background and how they behave in personal interviews, *not* how they perform. Employment vetting does not include auditions. Unfortunately, when businesspeople stand up in front of an audience to present, the adrenaline rush causes them to exhibit negative behavior that produces a negative perception and defeats their own cause.

The preceding examples vividly illustrate the *presenter behavior/ audience perception* relationship.

- When the deer in the headlights presenter's hand trembled, you felt it.
- When the presenter stepped into the bright light and squinted, you winced.
- When the couples in the British study saw each other shocked, their mirror neurons caused them to respond just as they did when they were shocked themselves.
- When *Nova*'s Robert Krulwich struggled and strained with a stack of heavy boxes, complete strangers on the street reflected his strain.
- When Bob Dole spoke inspirational words, the voters were not inspired.
- When Gray Davis was outshone by Arnold Schwarzenegger, he lost his governorship.

All these examples represent *negative* behavior that produced *negative* perceptions. Now flip the lens: When the behavior is *positive*, it produces a *positive* perception.

For a case in this point, let's go back to July 27, 2004, at the Democratic National Convention. Barack Obama, a then-unknown

42-year-old state legislator from Illinois, stood and delivered a stirring keynote speech that concluded with these words:

America, tonight, if you feel the same energy that I do, if you feel the same urgency that I do, if you feel the same passion that I do, if you feel the same hopefulness that I do, if we do what we must do, then I have no doubt that all across the country, from Florida to Oregon, from Washington to Maine, the people will rise up in November, and John Kerry will be sworn in as president. And John Edwards will be sworn in as vice president. And this country will reclaim its promise. And out of this long political darkness a brighter day will come.[6]

Obama expressed the energy, urgency, and passion that he felt, with great energy, urgency, and passion in his voice and body (Video Frame 2.2).

Video Frame 2.2 Barack Obama at the 2004 Democratic National Convention

Note

To see this live video clip from Barack Obama's speech with commentary, please visit www.powerltd.com/tpp and use the pass code you saw in the introduction.

The delivery system lifted the payload into orbit and the convention delegates at the packed Fleet Center in Boston rose in unison to give Obama an enthusiastic ovation. For days and weeks afterward, the media was filled with glowing praise for the charismatic young politician, making him an overnight star. Three months later, he swept into office as a first-term U.S. senator by 70 percent, the widest margin ever in an Illinois Senate race.[7] Four years later, his momentum unabated, Barack Obama became, and four months after that, the 44th president of the United States the Democratic presidential candidate—all launched by just one 16-minute, 25-second speech.

Note

You'll find a fuller analysis of Barack Obama's technique and style in chapter 10.

The Effectiveness Matrix

From all of the foregoing you can draw conclusions about the effectiveness of both the story and the delivery. In the matrix shown in Figure 2.2, the story effectiveness is charted on the vertical axis from low *up* to high, and the delivery effectiveness is charted on the horizontal axis from low *out* to high.

A presenter can be in one of four quadrants:

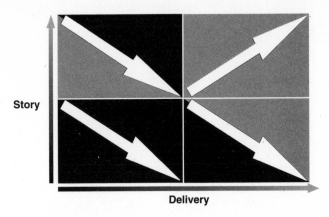

Figure 2.2   Effectiveness Matrix

- *Lower left: low story, low delivery.* Think of a little boy caught with his hand in the cookie jar. As he protests, "I was just looking for my homework, Mommy!" his eyes roll skyward, and his body, arms, and legs squirm and fidget like a Mexican jumping bean.
- *Lower right: high delivery driven down by low story.* Think of a holy roller striding about the stage grandly, gesturing flamboyantly, and bellowing in stentorian tones, "Brothers and Sisters, send me your life savings and I'll save your souls!"
- *Upper left: high story driven down by low delivery.* Think of Bob Dole murmuring, "My heart is buoyant."
- *Upper right: high story, high delivery.* Ideal.

Why, then, isn't every presenter or speaker in the upper-right-hand quadrant, by default? Why can't we launch our valuable payload with the most powerful delivery system? The reason is that when every human being stands up in front of an audience at the Moment of Truth, each of us is impacted by an onslaught of forces that are seemingly above and beyond our control. Including me, and I have been presenting for two decades.

In the following chapters, you will learn what those forces are and how you can *indeed* control each of them. Let's begin by looking more deeply into the most powerful of those forces: the Fight-or-Flight Syndrome.

CHAPTER

3

The Butterflies in Your Stomach

*There are two types of speakers: those who get nervous and those
who are liars.*

—Mark Twain

Fight-or-Flight

Every living being on the planet, from one-celled organisms to four-
legged animals to two-legged humans, responds to imminent danger
by standing its ground and fighting for its life or by fleeing for its life.
To enable either of these reactions, the body releases a sudden spurt of
adrenaline and activates the sympathetic nervous system. This vast
internal emergency network then sets many parts of the body into
accelerated motion:

- *Eyes:* Pupils dilate to increase the field of vision.
- *Heart:* Pumps faster to send blood to the extremities to flail in
  defense or to run to safety.

- *Blood pressure*: Elevates due to increased blood flow.
- *Blood sugar levels*: Elevate to generate more energy.
- *Lungs*: Increase respiration rate to put more oxygen into the blood.
- *Sweat glands*: Activate to avoid overheating.
- *Salivary glands*: Shut down to suspend digestion.
- *Limbs*: Primed to Fight-or-Flight.

Law enforcement officers, when interrogating suspects—a Fight-or-Flight situation if there ever were one—use polygraphs or lie detectors to monitor the telltale physiological functions of stress: heart rate, blood pressure, respiratory rate, and skin conductivity for perspiration.

The Limbs

When a four-legged animal senses imminent danger, it scampers away to escape: the Flight reaction. When a four-legged animal can't escape because it is trapped in the back of the cave, it will lash out at its attacker: the Fight reaction. In addition to lashing out, the animal will also protect its underbelly, the vulnerable part of the body that contains the vital organs. When a dog or a cat feels threatened, it hunkers down to the ground, contracting its fore and hind paws. In other words, the adrenaline rush sends a powerful signal to the limbs.

When a two-legged animal senses imminent danger, its limbs respond instinctively to flee: the Flight reaction; or it puts up its dukes: the Fight reaction.

When a two-legged presenting animal is faced with the daunting task of standing exposed before an audience, the solitary focus of attention for dozens, if not hundreds or thousands of watchful eyes, it responds with the Flight reaction: pacing around the platform like a caged tiger. When a two-legged presenting animal cannot escape because it is trapped by the microphone, the computer, the lectern—and the expectant audience—it responds by protecting its vulnerable

Photograph 3.1   *September Morn* by Paul Chabas, 1912

underbelly with its limbs. Of course, the civilized presenter is not going to strike the pose in the famous painting, *September Morn* (Photograph 3.1)

But the two-legged presenting animal does perform variations of *September Morn*:

- Hands clasped below the waist in front (the "fig leaf").
- Hands clasped behind the back (the "reverse fig leaf").
- Both hands tightly clasped above the waist.
- Half-clasped (one hand pressed to the side defensively while the other hand gestures).
- Reverse half-clasped (the opposite hand pressed defensively to the side while the other hand gestures).
- One or both hands plunged deeply into the pants pockets.
- Both hands clenched as if in prayer.
- Both hands wringing in the manner of Lady Macbeth.
- Both hands cupped together, while the fingers of one hand nervously twirl the ring on the finger of the other hand.

- The fingers of both hands playing cat's cradle.
- The fingers of both hands forming an Indian tepee with the fingertips in what is known as "a butterfly doing pushups on a mirror."

The common factor in all these movements is that the upper arms press tightly against the side of the body, positioning the forearms and hands to be able to quickly dart down to protect the vulnerable underbelly. As a result, the elbows clasp the body as if they were attached by Velcro. All these positions have one common name: *body wrap.*

At the same time the arms are wrapping the body, many other parts of the body go into action simultaneously:

- *The eyes* sweep the room frantically in search of escape routes— "How do I get out of here?"
- *The heart* pumps faster to rush blood to the extremities.
- *The hydraulic system* screeches into reverse: The palms, usually dry, get clammy from perspiration, cooling the rush of warm blood, and the mouth, usually moistened by the salivary glands, goes bone dry.
- *The nerve synapses* fire off more rapidly to heighten alertness.

All these accelerated actions distort the presenter's senses into *time warp.*

Time Warp

Time moves very differently for a person standing in front of a roomful of people. Even for me.

You'll recall from the preface that, before becoming a presentations coach, I was a producer of public affairs programs for WCBS-TV. Television people live by the clock. I still wear a chronograph, even though I've been out of the business for two decades. Counting time is easy for me; I can easily calculate backward and forward in units of 60, but I have difficulty balancing my checkbook.

For nearly all the time since I left broadcasting, I have been a presentations coach, and almost every business day, I present material that is quite familiar to me. As a result, my adrenaline flow is only modestly elevated when I am in front of an audience.

With that as background, I had occasion to return to a television studio after a prolonged absence during the promotional media tour for my first book, *Presenting to Win* (Financial Times, 2003). Before the video taping began, as an audio technician attached my microphone, the interviewer chatted amiably with me. I asked her how long the interview would last, and she replied, "Oh, about four or five minutes."

Soon the stage manager cued the interviewer to start the actual interview. Our conversation continued smoothly, but suddenly, all *too* suddenly, the interviewer said, "We're about out of time. Thank you, Jerry, for joining us here today."

As the technician returned to remove my microphone, I asked the interviewer, "Did you run out of time?"

"Why?" she asked.

"You cut me off after only a couple of minutes."

"No," she replied, and then called into the control room, "George, how long did that piece run?"

A moment later, the disembodied voice of George boomed out over a loudspeaker, "Four minutes and forty-six seconds."

Four minutes and forty-six seconds felt like a couple of minutes! A 150 percent misperception of time! And I know time, I know television, and I present almost daily! Imagine the degree of mis-perception for anyone who presents less frequently.

That's time warp.

Adrenaline-Driven Behavior/Audience Perception

Here's how all the preceding *involuntary* presenter behavior, gathering momentum in a rolling chain action, impacts audience perception:

- *Eyes*: Rapid movement appears shifty-eyed or *furtive*. The same action causes:
  - *Head*: Sweeping back and forth, appears *harried*.
  - *Hands and arms*: Body wrap appears *defensive*, as in Photograph 3.2.
- The defensiveness freezes the presenter into the deer in the headlights pose, immobilizing the *features*, which appear *fearful*; also making the *posture* rigid, which appears *protective*. Moreover,

(Photo by Rich Hall)

Photograph 3.2 Body Wrap

by pressing the arms against the rib cage, the air supply in the lungs is constricted, which, in turn, impacts:

- *Voice*: Low *volume* sounds *weak*; and narrow *inflection* sounds *monotonous*.
- *Vital organs*: The heart, lungs, and synapses accelerate into time warp, which also impacts:
  - Cadence: Rapid *tempo* sounds *rushed*; and crams the words into a steady flat line *pattern*, resulting in a *data dump* that makes it difficult for the audience to separate ideas; the steady pattern also causes **unwords** ("um" or "ah") to intrude repeatedly, which sounds *uncertain*.

The Moment of Truth

All these powerful forces surging around inside your body and your mind—and reverberating throughout your audience—occur at the critical juncture of the Moment of Truth. But that moment is preceded by many other moments that stretch all the way back to another important moment: when the date and time for your mission-critical presentation is set.

As the clock starts ticking down to D-day, you think, "How will I *ever* find the time to get it done?" Suddenly, you ignite a state of high anticipation that builds in intensity until the Moment of Truth; and then the sight of your live audience kicks your adrenaline flow even higher. Nip your anticipation in the bud. Diminish your anxiety by taking charge of your content in its *preparation*, the subject of the next chapter.

CHAPTER

4

How to Prepare Your Content

The Seven Steps of Story Development

The problem is that nobody knows how to tell a story. And what's worse, nobody knows that they don't know how to tell a story.

—Don Valentine,
founding partner, Sequoia Capital;
original investor: Apple Computer, Oracle, Cisco Systems, Yahoo!,
Google

Many presenters and speakers, pressured by the demands of business and daily life, often beg, borrow, or steal a colleague's material or put off their own preparation until the eleventh hour. Either choice serves to create anxiety during the delay. Worse still, both choices result in an excessive dump of disorganized data during your presentation. Predictably, your audience will react with puzzlement, boredom, or restlessness; any of which, when perceived by you, will heighten your anxiety. Your stress level will increase and you'll find it

35

harder to be confident, relaxed, and persuasive. Break the vicious cycle by preparing in advance. Your presentation will be much stronger if you spend enough time to organize, develop, and think through your content.

Do the data dump during your *preparation* and not during your *presentation*. During the preparation, clear your mind by eliminating all the superfluous material and identifying the essential. The Power Presentations story development process is described in detail in my previous book, *Presenting to Win*, but for your convenience, I have condensed the process here into seven steps.

The Seven Steps of Story Development

1. Establish the Framework of Your Presentation

Define the playing field. Every sport sets the fair and foul bounds for the game. The same definition is necessary in presentations and speeches. Without boundaries, you tend to throw everything into the mix and your story becomes a confusing assault on your audience.

Consider your story as a blank white frame. Along one border, identify the objective of your presentation—your call to action—and its supporting points. On the other side, analyze your target audience: who they are, where they stand, what they know, and what they need to know in order to respond to your call to action. Your call to action is also known as *Point B*. Point B assumes that you have thoroughly analyzed your audience's position—consider that Point A—and have determined what you have to tell them to get them to move to your position, Point B. That movement is the essence of persuasion.

When you fill in each side of the outer frame with this pertinent data, you define the scope and context of your story.

Note

The Power Presentations Framework form is available for download from our Web site: www.powerltd.com/tpp.

Now, with the playing field set, you can move into the smaller, more focused area in the center of the frame and start brainstorming the key elements of your story.

2. Brainstorming: Consider All the Possibilities

Although you have established the framework of one particular presentation to one particular target audience, you still have a welter of supporting and related ideas ricocheting around in your mind. Get them out of your mind and look at them in an objective, panoramic view. Write your ideas on paper, a computer, Post-its, or a whiteboard. In my days as a television producer, as we developed our programs and documentaries, we wrote our ideas on 3 × 5 index cards and mounted them on a cork board with push-pins. Write all your ideas in the center of your Framework form.

The purpose of this part of the process is to lay out all the possible ideas you might consider and then evaluate, select, or reject each idea. Separate the wheat from the chaff. As you proceed, arrange the remaining kernels into related groups. Distill all your ideas into a few main themes. Brainstorming all of your ideas to find the essential ones is very similar to the way musicians use improvisation to find their main musical themes.

3. Roman Columns: Find a Mnemonic Device for Your Main Themes

If you visit Rome today and tour the ruins of the great Forum, you are likely to hear your guide describe the glory days of the Roman Empire, around 100 BCE. You are also likely hear the guide talk about the classic Roman orators who spoke in the Forum for hours on end without any notes. Paper had not yet been invented. To help them remember what to say, the orators used the stately marble columns of the Forum as prompts. As Cicero and his colleagues strode around delivering their rhetoric, they would stop at individual columns to discourse on particular themes. Each column represented the focal point for a cluster of subordinate or related ideas.

Two millennia later, the Roman column concept has taken on a life of its own. If you do an Internet search for "Roman room memory," you will find more than a quarter of a million entries describing variations of Cicero's method; most of them propose using pieces of furniture in a room as reminders of specific points in a sequence.

Will Poole, a corporate vice president in Microsoft's Unlimited Potential Group, encountered another disciple of Cicero. When I introduced the Roman column concept to Will, it reminded him of an incident in India where he was being taken on a tour of a temple. Will asked his guide a question about an area of the temple they had just left, but the guide replied that he couldn't answer that question unless he returned to that area.

While the Roman orators and Will Poole's guide used columns or Indian temple objects as memory triggers, the Roman column concept can serve as your aid to distill your story into a few succinct primary themes. These mnemonics will lighten your mental—and, in turn, adrenal—load. The object of your brainstorming is to develop the Roman columns of your own story; about five or six in all is optimal.

4. Flow Structure: Provide a Road Map for Your Audience and for You

The five or six Roman columns need a logical sequence so that your audience can follow you, but also so that *you* know where *you* are going. You can provide both of these benefits by integrating all your Roman columns within an overarching road map. Envelop your main themes within a larger unit. Give the individual components of your story a meaningful, orderly flow. Professional writers, particularly novelists, playwrights, and screenwriters, call this the *story arc*. You can create an arc for your presentation or speech by encompassing your Roman columns within a logical template known as a Flow Structure. There are 16 different Flow Structures described in *Presenting to Win*. Choose one or two for your entire presentation. Two of the simplest and most common are:

- *Chronological.* Track your story along a timeline: past, present, and future; yesterday, today, and tomorrow; year over year.
- *Numerical.* Combine all your Roman columns and assign them a number, as David Letterman does with his nightly "Top Ten," or as Stephen Covey did in his *Seven Habits of Highly Effective People*. Then count down for your audience as you discuss each column.

> **Note**
>
> This chapter is a composite of those two Flow Structures: Chronological (the temporal progression of the story development process) and Numerical (seven steps).

With less baggage to carry up to the lectern and a defined road map, your mind will be clear and your adrenaline flow will diminish. This effective mental step can have an immediate positive physical effect on your delivery, as evidenced by the story of Jeff Raikes.

Jeff, until his recent retirement to become the CEO of the Bill and Melinda Gates Foundation, was the president of the Microsoft Business Division. Jeff was with Microsoft for 27 years and was one of the corporation's major spokesmen. I had the privilege of working with him earlier in his career, in 1991, when he was a junior executive.

At the time, Jeff was developing a presentation to introduce a new product and asked me to coach him. I offered him the full three-day Power Presentations program, which covers the full gamut of skills from story development through to delivery skills; but Jeff was pressed for time and could only afford to spend one day. In that one day, all we did was to work through the four preceding steps: identifying his Point B, analyzing his audience; defining his key ideas, discarding the unnecessary ones; and then putting his final choices into a logical sequence.

Jeff then went off and gave his presentation. Afterward, an account executive at Waggener Edstrom, Microsoft's public relations agency, called me to praise Jeff's dynamic delivery. But in our one day together, I had not mentioned a single word about Jeff's body language or voice! His clarity of mind had given him the comfort level to present with confidence.

5. Graphics: Use Visual Aids

Please note how far into the development process we have come before I brought up graphics, relegating them to a position subordinate to the story. Unfortunately, in common practice, the opposite is true. Most presentation development starts with a frantic aggregation and shuffling of existing slides. This ultimately results in a visual data dump with no clear flow. By starting with the story instead, the graphics then assume their proper role: as support of the narrative.

PowerPoint has become the *lingua franca* of twenty-first-century communications, ranging from grade-school rooms all the way up to boardrooms; but is all too often used as a visual hindrance rather than a visual aid. The simple solution is to design all your graphics with the Less Is More principle. You can find specific details to implement this vital principle in *Presenting to Win*.

6. Ownership: Don't Pass the Buck

Buffeted by the daily pressures of business, far too many presenters take the shortcut of appropriating their colleagues' slides, or offloading the presentation to the marketing department or to an administrative assistant, or sending the whole job to a professional production house. Each of these approaches results in an "I wonder what *that* means?" reaction from the presenter when the outsourced slides appear. Instead, take charge of your own presentation.

This is not to say that you must execute each and every step of each and every presentation, but do become a hands-on presenter and supervise its development at pivotal points. When D-day arrives, you will not incur any unpleasant surprises.

7. Verbalization: Practice the Right Way

Clarity of mind comes from clarification of content, but focusing your major ideas is only the first step. You can generate even more ease of mind by a practice methodology known as *Verbalization*. This useful technique simply means that, in your rehearsals, you speak the *actual* words of your presentation or speech *aloud*, just the way you will do it when you are in front of your intended audience.

Verbalization crystallizes ideas. In daily human communication we often seek face-to-face meetings with both personal and business associates to talk things out. Businesspeople and diplomats negotiate back and forth until they achieve win-win agreements. Professional writers often read their work aloud to themselves to hear how it sounds and clarify the flow. Clearly, Verbalization works.

Yet, for some inexplicable reason, presenters and speakers are reluctant to Verbalize. They find it either boring or tedious or time-consuming, and they relegate one of the most powerful techniques to one of the most underutilized. In doing so, they lose a golden opportunity to gain control over their content. Most people are willing to endure repetitive physical training to build their muscles and skills as athletes; Verbalization is the mental equivalent of building your intellectual muscles and narrative skills.

> **Note**
>
> This is *not* to say that you should Verbalize to the point of memorization. Memorization is fitting for the timeless words of William Shakespeare and other professional writers, but it is
>
> *(continued)*

unnecessary for presentations and speeches. In fact, memorization can be counterproductive. If you commit specific word strings to memory and then lose just one word during your presentation, you will become completely unhinged. Never memorize. Verbalize only until you have a strong *sense* of your flow.

I practice what I preach. As a professional coach, I present almost daily with content that I have developed and have been delivering for over 20 years. I don't Verbalize the material for my daily sessions, but when I introduce new material or create new content for special events, I often Verbalize as many as a dozen times.

I did this for a keynote speech I was to deliver at an investment banking conference. The process worked and the speech went flawlessly. However, immediately after the speech, I had to record excerpts for a promotional video. There were only about a dozen very short excerpts, again drawn from the body of quite familiar material, but I hadn't Verbalized the excerpts and, because the material was out of context, I stumbled frequently during the recording. (Fortunately, the video editor was merciful and saved only the good takes.) I learned my lesson, and since then, have never presented in *any* new situation without first Verbalizing.

I am not alone. Patrick McGovern is the founder and chairman of International Data Group (IDG), the world's largest technology media, research, and event company. IDG published the successful series of *Dummies* books (until the company sold that unit to John Wiley & Sons, Inc., in 2001.) In an article in the *Wall Street Journal* about Mr. McGovern, he revealed that he kept a lifelike dummy of himself in his office. The article explained that, ". . . he can crystallize his thoughts by speaking an idea aloud to the dummy."[1]

With these seven steps providing a solid foundation for your ease of mind, you are now ready to step up to the front of the room to face the Moment of Truth. As you approach the platform, however, you must do so with the proper frame of mind. Athletic coaches call this "PMA," or Positive Mental Attitude, which means approaching the execution of a sport affirmatively. Unfortunately, there is a pervasive belief in the presentation trade that "good speakers are born, not made." This is an NMA, or negative mental attitude, which implies that change is impossible.

Let us dispel that notion once and for all in the next chapter.

CHAPTER
5

You *Can* Be a Power Presenter—Charisma *Not* Required

Ya either got it, or ya ain't. And, boys, I got it!
—Stephen Sondheim
"Rose's Turn" lyrics from *Gypsy*

I n my two decades as a speaking coach, one of the most frequent assertions I've heard is, "Good speakers are born, not made," and its extended variation, "That person has natural charisma." The corollary implication of this view is "Change is impossible." You either have it or you do not. Nature nullifies Nurture. For some unearthly reason, many people cling to this preconception, and recite it, almost as a pledge of allegiance. The pledge persists despite overwhelming evidence and advice to the contrary from every corner and every walk of life, ranging from grade school at the low end to psychiatry at the high end. Change *is* possible for *anyone.*

A case in point comes from President George W. Bush. During his first run for office in 2000, Mr. Bush's chronic difficulty with the English language made him the frequent butt of jokes in the media and the endless target of the late-night comedians. The nadir of his verbal trouble came on September 12, 2000, during the heat of battle of his campaign for the presidency.

In the previous week, the Republican National Committee had run a television commercial in which the word *RATS* allegedly flashed on screen for a split second before the full word *Bureaucrats* (a thinly veiled reference to Democrats) appeared. The Democrats accused the Republicans of dirty tricks and the press immediately seized on the controversy. When then-Governor Bush made a campaign stop at the airport in Orlando, Florida, he was confronted about the issue during a press conference.

The candidate responded effectively with his prepared position, but when he referred to the implied manipulation of the film, he called it "subliminable."[1] A few moments later, he repeated the mispronunciation. Moments later, he repeated it twice more. The reporters on the scene picked up on it. One of them suggested that the cause of the governor's chronic mispronunciations and malapropisms might be dyslexia.

To make matters worse, as Mr. Bush fielded the journalists' challenging questions, his Visual element worked against him. Standing on the tarmac, with his head inclined toward the phalanx of his inquisitors, he appeared hunched over. In that defensive stance, the collar of his jacket pulled away and made his suit look ill-fitting. And as he peered into the forest of cameras and microphones pointed at him— and the midday sun overhead—he squinted his eyes and furrowed his eyebrows, two facial characteristics that had become another target of satire for those late-night comedians.

Vainly, Mr. Bush tried to defend himself, saying, "It's amazing what happens when you run for president!" (Video Frame 5.1).

Video Frame 5.1 Governor George W. Bush Responds to Charges of Subliminal Advertising.

Note

To see this live video clip from George W. Bush's press conference with commentary, please visit www.powerltd.com/tpp and use the pass code you saw in the introduction.

Four months later, on January 20, 2001, when he assumed his office, the victorious George W. Bush was a changed man. As he delivered his first inaugural address, he stood erect in the chilly drizzle of a wintry Washington day. His smartly tailored dark overcoat sparkled with droplets of mist. He held his head high, and his eyes, despite their innate narrow configuration, were now set in a determined, steely glint that added import to the concluding words of his speech (Video Frame 5.2).

Video Frame 5.2   President George W. Bush, First Inaugural Address

Note

To see this live video clip from George W. Bush's Inaugural Address with commentary, please visit www.powerltd.com/tpp and use the pass code you saw in the introduction.

Our duty is fulfilled in service to one another. Never tiring, never yielding, never finishing. We renew that purpose today: to make our country more just and generous, to affirm the dignity in our lives and every life. This work continues, the story goes on, and an angel still rides in the whirlwind and directs this storm. God bless you all and God bless America.[2]

Over the course of a few months, George W. Bush was able to change, to make a significant improvement. In fact, he continued to improve further throughout his presidency. As you will see in chapter 8, he proceeded to gain control of other important aspects of his presentation skills.

Mr. Bush's predecessor, Bill Clinton, with his usual rhetorical flair and an established reputation as a superstar of the keynote circuit, seemingly did not need any makeovers. Clinton is often called "a natural," or "gifted," variations of the label that is often applied to charismatic speakers. But Mr. Clinton was not born with this capability.

He admits as much in his autobiography, calling his first speech effort while in high school "unremarkable."[3] He was still far less than remarkable in 1988 when, as the governor of Arkansas, he gave a nominating speech for Michael Dukakis at the Democratic National Convention in Atlanta. Here is how the *New York Times* described his performance:

Mr. Clinton was given the entire 15 minutes allowed by the rules, with no seconding speeches to compete with. For reasons that few here could fathom, he prepared an 18-page speech, far too long, and read almost every word of it in a damp style that lost his audience within the first couple of minutes.

He plowed on through signals from the chairman and House Speaker, Jim Wright of Texas, to desist, through the frantic flashing of a red light in front of him, through the gestures of many in the front rows, who drew their index fingers across their throats in the broadcast symbol for "cut it short."[4]

Clinton rambled on for so long that the delegates began to chant, "We want Mike!" And when he finally said, "In closing . . ." the crowd roared their approval.

Note

To see this live video clip from Bill Clinton's speech, please visit www.powerltd.com/tpp and use the pass code you saw in the introduction.

In his autobiography, Clinton confessed, "It was 32 minutes of total disaster."[5]

Nor was he very charismatic in 1995 when, at the start of his third year as president, he delivered a rambling State of the Union address. The laundry list of a speech ran 81 minutes, the longest in history.

Clearly, Clinton changed, and it is very likely that his change began as a result of two pivotal moments that occurred very close to each other and very early on in his life, involving two of history's most charismatic speakers. On July 24, 1963, as part of a student government group visiting the White House, the 16-year-old Bill Clinton got to shake the hand of President John F. Kennedy and have the moment preserved for posterity in an historic photograph (Photograph 5.1).

Photograph 5.1   Sixteen-Year-Old Bill Clinton Meets President John F. Kennedy

Thirty-five days later, the young Clinton sat in front of a television set at home, watching the Reverend Martin Luther King, Jr. deliver his towering "I Have a Dream" speech, which the mature Clinton was later to call "the greatest speech of my lifetime."[6]

Surely, when Clinton had watched Kennedy deliver his classic inaugural address two years earlier, he saw Kennedy's forearm repeatedly punch the air with the four fingers of his hand curled in to his palm while his thumb rested on top (Video Frame 5.3).

Video Frame 5.3 President John F. Kennedy Delivering His Inaugural Address

Note

This live video clip from John F. Kennedy's gesture is compared with Bill Clinton's gesture in a split screen in the next video frame 5.4.

The vigorous gesture, which was to become Kennedy's trademark, has since been likened to inserting a credit card in a slot. And, surely, if you watch Clinton speak today, you will see him use that same credit card gesture, with his thumb held just a little higher.

At the Democratic National Convention in Los Angeles on August 14, 2000, the party was about to name Vice President Al Gore as their standard bearer, but they took the time to say goodbye to the outgoing president. In a production only Hollywood could mount, a battery of television cameras tracked Clinton's arrival, transmitting his image onto giant screens inside the Los Angeles Convention Center and outside to a global television audience. A mobile camera followed him striding through the corridors beneath the arena, up a long ramp and onto the main stage. It was a theatrical entrance straight out of *Rocky*.

By the time Clinton reached the rostrum, the admiring delegates in the arena were at a fever pitch of anticipation. He did not disappoint them. Leaning toward the audience, he dipped his head, pursed his lips, and softened his voice.

My friends, 54 years ago this week I was born in a summer storm to a young widow in a small southern town. America gave me the chance to live my dreams. And I have tried as hard as I knew how to give you a better chance to live yours.

His head bobbing, his face radiant, his eyes shining, Clinton poured on the charm.

Now my hair's a little grayer, my wrinkles are a little deeper, but with the same optimism and hope I brought to the work I loved so eight years ago, I want you to know my heart is filled with gratitude.

He clutched his hand to his heart, and then shook his head from side to side.

My fellow Americans, the future of our country is now in your hands.

Clinton opened his palms to the audience.

You must think hard . . .

Now he raised one crooked finger.

. . . feel deeply . . .

He opened all his fingers fully and turned his hand to clutch his heart.

. . . and choose wisely. And remember . . .

The crooked forefinger came up again and wagged from side to side.

. . . whenever you think about me, keep putting people first.

Now he retracted the crooked forefinger and replaced it with his own version of the Kennedy gesture: his thumb upraised and the other four fingers of his hand curled into his palm (Video Frame 5.4).

Video Frame 5.4   Bill Clinton, Farewell Speech in 2000.

Note

To see this live video clip from Bill Clinton's speech with commentary, please visit www.powerltd.com/tpp and use the pass code you saw in the introduction.

As Clinton spoke the next four words, he beat his cadence with that extended thumb.

Keep . . . building . . . those . . . bridges.

Moving deftly, he switched back to the crooked forefinger and, using it like the baton of a maestro, continued to stroke the word-for-word cadence. In perfect harmony with the rhythm, his voice rose in crescendo until it punctuated the final syllable of the final distended word.

And don't . . . stop . . . thinking . . . about . . . to-mor-row!

His other hand came up to his temple for an instant and then flung out to the crowd in a majestic military-style salute to accompany his last words.

I love you, and good night![7]

The delegates rose to their feet in wild jubilation, and Clinton rode off into his presidential sunset, with the thunderous cheers for his valedictory reverberating loudly through the Convention Center.

Five months later, Clinton left the White House and became a private citizen. Hardly skipping a beat, he hit the public speaking circuit. In his first year out of office, he earned $9.2 million; in the next year, $9.5 million. In the third year, his fees dropped to $4.4 million, but that was because he was busy writing his memoir for an advance of $15 million dollars. By 2006 he was back up to speed, earning $10 million dollars and continued at that pace in 2007 with another $10 million.[8,9] A vast difference from having been hooted off the podium 20 years earlier.

The point of this chapter is that change is indeed possible. Both George W. Bush and Bill Clinton were able to change. You can change, too. You are not doomed to eternal mediocrity. You may never ascend to the heights of a Clinton, Kennedy, or King, but you are certainly capable of change. Change your thinking and, as a result, control your behavior.

Have a positive mental attitude!

CHAPTER

6

The Mental Method of Presenting

Make the Butterflies Fly in Formation

The Power of the Mind

Sound mind, sound body.

—Juvenal (60–130 AD)

A sound mind in a sound body is a short, but full description of a happy state in this World: he that has these two has little more to wish for; and he that wants either of them will be little the better for anything else.

—John Locke (1632–1704)

Control of the mind, or *concentration*, is essential in every activity in the human experience. Even relaxation requires you to clear your mind of extraneous thoughts and focus on one tranquil image.

57

The mind plays a particularly important role in physical perform-ances, such as sports, music, dance, and theater. In fact, a form of acting known as "The Method" revolutionized the theatrical profession in the middle of the twentieth century by breaking ranks with the theretofore traditional emphasis on vocal projection and body movement and focusing instead on emotions. It was this very revolution that inspired me to break ranks with the traditional presentation skills emphasis on voice and body language and focus instead on the mind.

I spent my early days as a freelance presentation coach inflicting the rigors of a close-order drill on unwilling and unsuspecting business-people just like you, acting as a trainer, treating my clients as perform-ers. I spent entire sessions telling people what to do and what not to do with their voices and body language. I badgered them to speak faster or slower, louder or softer, or to make their gestures wider or narrower or bigger or smaller. At the end of the day, I was able to change their behavior infinitesimally, only to see them go out into the real world and rapidly regress to a point further back from where I had started with them at the beginning of the day.

What's wrong with this picture? A presentation coach is supposed to provide service, not *disservice*. As I began to develop my own business, I knew that dealing with the adrenaline rush would require a radically different approach. Ironically, the approach I chose came from a source that was 180 degrees from the corporate path on which I was headed: acting in the theater.

The Method was based on ideas pioneered by Constantine Sta-nislavski (1863–1938), the director of the Moscow Art Theater. Stanislavski's seminal book, *An Actor Prepares*, influenced an artists' collective in New York called the Group Theatre and its offshoot, the Actors Studio. The Studio, as it came to be known, went on to develop The Method and propagate it widely. In the process, the Studio became the spawning ground for legions of luminaries, among them Marlon Brando, Paul Newman, James Dean, Marilyn Monroe, and Robert DeNiro.

Simply stated, The Method rejected the long-established theater practice in which actions are deliberately staged to depict emotions, and reversed field to have emotions drive actions. To achieve this, Method actors use concentration to recall sense memories of events in their own lives to evoke feelings that help them create realistic depictions of the characters they portray.

However, you are not reading this book to learn about being anyone other than yourself, and it is unlikely that you will purse a career in acting (other than in your community theater), so let's focus instead on how concentration is employed in a far more relevant area: athletics. Think about your sport of choice, be it skiing, tennis, golf, swimming, basketball, or soccer; in each of them, concentration is fundamental. In each of them, the mind is used to control the body.

Well, it happens to be the very same mind and the very same body that you use when you stand in front of an audience to present or to make a speech. Therefore, use your mind to control your physical delivery of your message. Use concentration to conquer your adrenaline rush—*and* your audience. Apply the Mental Method of Presenting.

It works. Ever since I broke ranks with the drill sergeant approach to delivery skills and shifted to the Mental Method, I began to produce positive results in presenters and speakers. I have battle-tested and refined this technique for two decades with thousands of private clients, and now offer them to you.

What Was Going through Your Mind?

During coaching sessions with my clients, I ask each participant to stand and deliver a brief presentation to the other participants in the room—their colleagues—while we record the presentation on a digital video camera, an intentionally adrenaline-inducing scenario. As soon as each person concludes, I ask that person, "What were you thinking?

What was going through your mind as you were speaking?" Most of the time, most of the people say the same kinds of things.

"I was thinking about what I was saying."

"I was wondering what to do with my hands."

"I was trying to make eye contact with the audience."

"I was trying to get my point across."

"I was trying to slow down."

"I was nervous."

"I was trying to remember what to say next."

"I wished I'd practiced more."

All these statements have a least-common denominator: "How am *I* doing?" Put another way, the speakers were thinking, "Uh-oh! They're all looking at me!" "I'm on the spot!" "I'd better do well!" This mind-set serves only to heighten their—and *your*—fear of public speaking.

The solution to this monocular self-consciousness is to slam on the brakes and reverse gears. Do a sharp U-turn. Change the mind-set. Think instead, "How are *you* doing?" How is your audience doing? *Shift the focus from yourself to your audience.* This shift will not only reduce your anxiety, it will also heighten the effectiveness of your presentation or speech. That is the essence of the Mental Method of Presenting.

Concentration

The pivotal factor in this shift is concentration. Concentration is the primary factor for success in any physical endeavor, particularly sports. Ever since Juvenal we have been aware of the power of the mind to influence the body. In sports, concentration ranks higher in importance than conditioning, muscle mass, nutrition, hydration, or stamina.

Think of your own participatory sport and you will find that concentration is key: golf, tennis, swimming, basketball, biking, soccer, skiing, even running. Long-distance runners encounter what is known as the *wall*, a distant point in a race where racers feel completely spent and unable take another step. In marathon races, this phenomenon occurs somewhere around the twenty-third mile of the 26.3-mile course. Successful runners *do* take that next step: they go through the wall and they finish the race. They do it by sheer mental will alone. Electrolyte drinks or energy bars will not propel them forward; only their minds will.

Concentration is of paramount importance in skiing. To be effective, a skier must constantly focus on the proper positioning of body weight in relation to the slope of the hill. That factor became indelibly clear to me many years ago on a cold, clear January day in Vermont. I had been skiing vigorously all day and then took that one last run down the mountain. Exhilarated but fatigued, I got to the bottom of the hill and relaxed into my final turn. With my concentration off my skis, my weight shifted backward. The left ski caught on a mound, but I was moving too slowly to release the boot bindings. In that one instant, I tore the medial collateral ligament in my knee and ended my skiing days forever.

Concentration controls skis, racquets, clubs, balls, bats, oars, skates, sabers, weights, surfboards, bicycles—and the bodies that use them. Competitive athletes fully understand and appreciate this mind-body relationship. They strive for what is known as the *zone*, or what athletic coaches call *quiet mind*, a heightened state of mental and physical efficiency that produces peak performance. Professional and even amateur players spend substantial amounts of time and effort in quest of this exalted state.

- *Raise the bar.* To sharpen their concentration, some baseball players take batting practice with a bat half the diameter of a regulation bat. Some football players practice by trying to throw a ball through a rubber tire—as it swings suspended in midair. Raising the bar of difficulty forces the athlete to concentrate on the central factor, the ball.

- *Distraction*. Gymnasts develop their concentration during training by playing video games while their teammates shout at them. Before becoming a champion golfer, Tiger Woods's parents helped him to develop his concentration. His father jingled coins in his pocket during Tiger's practice sessions.

- *Meditation*. Tiger Woods's Buddhist mother taught him to focus by emptying his mind of extraneous thoughts. Today, his mental prowess is prominently featured on par with his athletic ability in a series of ads for Accenture.

- *Visualization*. Many athletes try to conjure a mental image of succeeding at their endeavor: crossing the goal line, envisioning the ball going where they want it to go, or their arrow hitting the bull's eye.

- *Neurofeedback*. This medical technique used to treat epilepsy and attention deficit hyperactivity disorder is now being tried by athletes. Electrodes that measure brainwaves are strapped onto the athletes' heads. They can then see their brainwave patterns on a screen and try to control the spikes with their concentration.[1]

- *Psychological consultation*. Dr. Bob Rotella, a sports psychologist, (one of about a thousand others in Division 47, an important subspecialty of the American Psychological Association) has developed a singular reputation as a coach to superstar athletes, entertainers, and executives. "Doc" focuses on the role of the mind in physical activity.

- *The Inner Game*. Doc Rotella owes a great deal, as do I, to the pioneering work of W. Timothy Gallwey, whose bestselling book, *The Inner Game of Tennis*, essentially established the field of sports psychology. This landmark work set the standard in sports by placing as much, if not more, emphasis on the mind as the body. Gallwey's own words state it best, "The inner game is the game that takes place in the mind of the player . . . it is played to overcome all habits of mind which inhibit excellence in performance."[2]

Universally in sports, the mind is used to control the body. It is the very same mind and the very same body that you use in presentations and speeches, so use your mind to control your body when you stand in front of an audience.

Concentrate.

The key in sports is to concentrate *outside* the body. Think of the *hill* in skiing, think of the *wind* in sailing, the *wave* in surfing, the *road* in auto racing; think of the *ball* in tennis, golf, volleyball, soccer, baseball, and basketball.

In presentations and speeches, think *outside* yourself; think outside your body, outside your hands and arms and eyes and voice, outside your story, outside your slides, outside your own mind. Think audience. Think on an even more granular level. Think about the equivalent of the ball in sports. Think about one person. Think about each and every person in your audience, one at a time.

This brings us directly to the foundation of the Mental Method: person-to-person conversation.

Conversation

It also brings us directly back to the question I posed at the very beginning of this book: Why would speaking, a most ordinary activity that most ordinary people practice every day with complete ease, become so fraught with dread when standing in front of an audience? The answer, as we now know, is the adrenaline rush that triggers the Fight-or-Flight Syndrome and sabotages the effective interpersonal dynamics we all employ so readily in ordinary conversation.

The challenge, then, when *you* are in front of an audience, is to re-create the conversational mode, the very mode in which most human beings are comfortable. To do this, let's first analyze the key dynamics of conversation. In any person-to-person exchange, the two parties:

- Make *eye* contact.
- Use their *hands* and *arms* to express themselves.
- Use their *voices* to punctuate their words.
- *Interact* by asking questions and exchanging ideas.

In presentations and speeches, the adrenaline rush causes drastic changes in each of those core elements:

- The *eyes* sweep the room furtively in search of escape routes.
- The *hands* and *arms* go into body wrap, constricting the lungs and causing:
  - The *voice* to become stifled because the air supply is reduced.
  - The *interaction* to grind to a halt. "Uh-oh! They're all looking at me!" "I'm on the spot!" "I'd better do well!"

But does the interaction *really* stop? If you see a person in your audience smiling at you in knowing appreciation, that's an interaction. If you see a person frowning at you in apparent disagreement, that's an interaction. If you see a person giving you a quizzical look, that's an interaction. If you see a person's head nodding in agreement, that's an interaction. So there *is* indeed interaction with your audience, but at the Moment of Truth, the interaction suddenly switches from verbal to nonverbal.

The challenge then is to focus on that pivotal instant, and make the nonverbal interaction work *for* you, rather than *against* you. And the way to do this is to shift from presentation mode to person-to-person conversation.

Person-to-Person

Whenever you step up to the front of a room to present or speak, regardless of the size of the audience—4, 40, 400, or 4,000—pick one person. It doesn't matter who: the person who greeted you at the door, someone you know, someone you don't know, a friendly face, or an unfriendly face. Pick only one person.

For an instant in time, set a new default: Presume that you and that individual are the only people present and, for that instant, disregard everyone else in the room. Make that person the object of your concentration. Then, as if the two of you were across a table or a desk, strike up a conversation.

You might even start by addressing that person by name, as you would in a conversation. Then continue to chat with that individual informally. When you chat, you don't *present*. You don't unload canned data unilaterally; you engage, you exchange, you think about the man or woman with whom you are chatting. You think about what he or she knows, about what he or she needs to know, and how he or she is receiving and reacting to what you are saying. This shift away from yourself and to that other person must be as deliberate as throwing an electric switch. Feel the *snap*.

Think "You"

As you converse with that one person, think about him or her as "you." This will orient your thinking farther away from yourself and further into the sphere of that other person. Think about the "you" in "How are *you* doing?" As you are thinking "you," say "you," too. Say "you" in a variety of ways:

- "The reason this is important to *you* is . . ."
- "What does this mean to *you*?"
- "Why am I telling *you* this?"
- "Let me show *you* . . ."

And the ultimate *"you"* phrase:

- "What's in it for *you*?"also known as WIIFY, a concept I introduced in *Presenting to Win*.

WIIFY is an *intentional* variation of the more common phrase "What's in it for me?" The shift from "me" to "you" is central to the Mental Method. WIIFY is the essential benefit statement in any presentation or speech. In my second book, *In the Line of Fire: How to Handle Tough Questions . . . When it Counts* (Pearson, 2005), I extended the value of the WIIFY concept to form an essential part of *Topspin*, the added-value conclusion to any answer. Topspin comes from the tennis term describing a power stroke that gives a player a winning advantage. In presentations, Topspin gives the presenter or speaker a winning advantage by adding a benefit in the form of a WIIFY, or by restating the call to action in the form of Point B. The Topspin icon is shown in Figure 6.1.

Think of the WIIFY as the ultimate form of Audience Advocacy; and think of the word "you" as the ultimate element of effective communication.

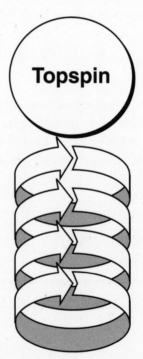

Figure 6.1 Topspin

If you search the Internet, you'll find tens of thousands of references to a Yale University study (unsubstantiated by Yale) ranking the 12 most persuasive words in the English language. *You* leads the list. Unsubstantiated or not, the power of *you* is best illustrated in the high-stakes world of politics.

In the run-up to the 2008 U.S. presidential election, Senator Hillary Rodham Clinton was the clear favorite in the Democratic Party, considered far and wide to be the presumptive nominee. Her closest challenger, among many, many others, was Senator Barack Obama. In mid-November 2007, a year before the election, and seven weeks before the first formal campaign test in the Iowa caucuses, the public opinion polls showed Senator Clinton in the lead, with 25 percent, and Senator Obama in third place, with 22 percent.[3]

Two weeks later, the *New Yorker* magazine ran a story about a change in Obama's campaign strategy:

Obama now tries to make a more personal connection with voters. In the past, he has been accused of making his campaign more about himself than about those who come to his rallies. Now the word "you" is mentioned as much as the word "I." "You're not heard. They're not listening to what you need," he told a crowd assembled at a rodeo site in Fort Madison on a recent evening. "You deserve a president who is thinking about you."[4]

Five weeks later, Obama won the Iowa caucuses with 37.6 percent of the vote, while Clinton placed third with at 29.5 percent.[5] On election night, after the final results, both of them spoke at their campaign headquarters, each for about the same length of time; yet each differed significantly in the number of times they said "you" or variations of "you," versus "I," as you can see in the table in Figure 6.2.[6]

	Clinton Concession	Obama Victory
"You"	17	26
"I"	35	10

Figure 6.2   "You" Versus "I" in the 2008 Iowa Post-Caucuses Speeches

Just to be sure that every single one of his words was absolutely correct, Senator Obama, alone among all the candidates, delivered his victory speech in Iowa with the aid of a teleprompter.[7]

Extending his affirmation of the power of *you* throughout the 2008 campaign, Obama's Web site displayed a banner across the top that read, "I'm asking *you* to believe. Not just in my ability to bring about real change in Washington . . . I'm asking *you* to believe in *yours*"[8] (italics mine).

> ## Note
>
> Chapter 10 has still further discussion of Barack Obama's winning style.

Keep the Think *you* approach firmly fixed in your mind. Start every one of your own speeches or presentations by snapping into the Mental Method. Pick one person in your audience, and then engage with that person as if you were in a conversation. Think "you" and say "you." Weave "you" throughout your words.

After an instant in time, shift your attention to another person, and strike up a conversation. Think about that person and make *you* statements to that person.

After another instant, shift to another person, and have another conversation. As you do, think "you" and say "you." Continue around the room in a series of person-to-person conversations.

One of the most striking and successful examples of the use of this person-to-person approach occurred at the 1996 Republican National Convention in San Diego. Bob Dole, the long-time Senate majority leader, was the presidential candidate. On the evening of August 14, his wife, Elizabeth, known popularly as Libby, made one of the nominating speeches. She came to the podium and began graciously:

Thank you so much ladies and gentlemen for the wonderful, warm welcome. And thank you Governor Wilson for your very kind words of introduction.

Now, you know tradition is that speakers at the Republican National Convention remain at this very imposing podium. But, tonight I'd like to break with tradition. For two reasons: One, I'm going to be speaking to friends and secondly I'm going to be speaking about the man I love, and it's just a lot more comfortable for me to do that down here with you.

With her well-chosen use of the word *you*, Libby Dole stepped away from the podium, picked up a wireless hand microphone, and walked down a short flight of steps onto the convention floor. From there she proceeded to move up and down the main aisle, stopping from time to time to chat with individuals who had been involved in some way with her husband. Each stop was a warm engagement, accompanied by embraces, hugs, and sometimes even a kiss (Video Frame 6.1).

The delegates loved it. They interrupted Libby Dole's tour de force repeatedly with applause and cheers. By the time she was ready to conclude, some 20 minutes later, she had every person in the Convention Center in the palm of her hand.

My fellow Americans . . .

Video Frame 6.1   Libby Dole at the Republican National Convention

> **Note**
>
> To see this live video clip from Libby Dole's speech with commentary, please visit www.powerltd.com/tpp and use the pass code you saw in the introduction.

Their applause and cheers were so loud Libby Dole had to pause for a moment. When they subsided, she resumed.

My fellow Americans, I believe that in the years to come, future generations will look back to this November and say here is where Americans earned a badge of honor. Here is where we elected the president who gave us more opportunities and smaller and more efficient government and stronger and safer families. Here is where we elected the better man who led us to a better America, because here is where we elected Bob Dole. God bless you all. Thank you.[9]

This is *not* to say that you should step away from your podium and walk out into the middle of your audience the way Libby Dole did, or as Oprah Winfrey does on her television program. Or as John Chambers, the CEO of Cisco Systems, often does in the business world. Mrs. Dole, Ms. Winfrey, and Mr. Chambers make their tours de force with the support of multiple video cameras projecting their walkabouts onto multiple giant screens.

You, a mere mortal, are not a performer. Nor should you attempt to be one. Simply be yourself. Be sincere. Be conversational. Remain at the front of the room; have your person-to-person engagements from there. Move around the room with your mind rather than your body. Use the Mental Method of Presenting.

Focus away from yourself, focus out, think *you*. Shift the focus from how you are doing to see how each person in your audience is doing. In the cinema, you often see a shot of a person in the foreground while the background is in soft focus. Suddenly, the camera shifts focus and the background becomes sharp, while the foreground goes soft. This shift calls attention to a new action. Create the same effect in your presentation: shift the focus from yourself to each member of your audience each time you engage.

When you make this outward shift, a powerful chain reaction begins. Each person you address directly will *see* the sincerity of your engagement and, therefore, they will *feel* engaged. This is the empathy dynamic you read about in chapter 2. The mirror neurons in the brain of every human being make them *feel* what they *see*. Remember how *you* felt the discomfort of the deer in the headlights presenter? Remember, too, that empathy is *involuntary*.

As you move around the room from person to person, each person you address directly will respond to you *involuntarily*. More often than not, their responses will be nonverbal.

Their responses will be manifested in facial expressions, body language, or head nods. Their facial expressions may be positive: a smile; or negative: a frown. Their body language may be positive: alert; or negative: slumped. Their head nods, however, will always be positive.

If you've ever gotten head nods from your audience, you'll know that there is no doubt whatsoever that it is positive. The head nods essentially tell you that that person is saying, "I got it!" Head nods represent the goal of every presenter and speaker: the magic moment known as A*ha!*

Better still, the head nods go right to the heart of your fear of public speaking: they tell you that your "performance" (that is, your execution—*not* your acting) is getting through to your audience. At that very moment, your brain, realizing that you are being effective, subconsciously concludes that neither Fight nor Flight is necessary. This mental realization transmits a physical signal to your adrenal gland, which promptly reduces the flow of adrenaline. Suddenly, the very behavior that enables organisms to survive in the wild—sweeping eyes, body wrap, accelerated heartbeat, pumping lungs, and rapidly firing synapses—abates.

Carly Simon, the popular singer and songwriter who admits to suffering from debilitating stage fright, has developed her own method to reduce anxiety by evoking responses from her audiences: "I'll pick out one person, usually in the first four rows, and sing a song directly to that person. He or she will get embarrassed and turn to people on his right or left . . . The focus I'm putting on him takes it directly away from me."[10]

While head nods rather than embarrassment are the desired reactions from your presentation audiences, Ms. Simon's approach does provide a related model for presenting. To reduce the fear of public speaking, you must shift your focus away from your concerns about your own success or failure and think about whether each and every individual in every audience is getting the message of your pitch. To paraphrase a core principle practiced by performers, you must work the room.

Therefore, head nods are the turning point. *Head nods are the endgame of the Mental Method of Presenting.*

How to Get Head Nods

Head nods are not mere happenstance. You can actually evoke them from your audience. To do so, you must take two specific action steps:

1. *Read the reaction of each person you are addressing.* Look to see if that person is getting it, or not getting it. If he or she is getting it, you will get head nods. If that person is not getting it, you will get a quizzical look or a frown.

2. *Respond to the reaction you observe by adjusting your content.* If you get head nods from one person, move on to engage with another person. If you get a frown or a quizzical look, *do* something about it:

   - Say it differently: "In other words . . ."
   - Explain your terms: "What that means is . . ."
   - Add depth: "Another way to look at this is . . ."
   - Define your acronyms: "That stands for . . ."
   - Give an example: "For instance, there is the case of . . ."
   - Provide evidence: "Research shows that . . ."
   - Customize: "Just before we started today, Bill asked . . ."
   - Elaborate: "Taking a deeper look at this . . ."
   - Add value: "The reason this is important to you is . . ." (a form of WIIFY)

You can also Adjust Your Content by addressing a person in the audience directly, inviting that person to explain his or her pensive or dubious expression. Say, for example, "You seem to have a question." However, this could make that person feel uncomfortable for having been singled out. The open question also invites a potentially digressive exchange or tangential discussion. It is far more powerful for you to react to such nonverbal signals *tacitly*, using one of the proactive phrase options preceding this paragraph. By making such seemingly unprompted connections, you create positive reactions from your audience *empathically*.

Whichever option you chose will very likely produce head nods from the person you have addressed. That positive interaction replicates person-to-person conversation, your comfort zone, and reduces your adrenaline flow.

While both Read the Reaction and Adjust Your Content are the pivotal techniques that will enable you to overcome your presentation anxiety and win over any audience, the latter is the more powerful of the two because the head nods that you produce in response to Adjusting Your Content provide a double benefit:

- You reduce your anxiety because the head nods tell you that you are being at effect rather than at risk.
- Your audience is gratified by your clarification of your content. Audience Advocacy at work.

Head nods are the endgame of the Mental Method of Presenting.

Most presenters present as if they are standing behind an invisible shield that separates and protects them from their audience. A select few presenters pierce the barrier and read their audience's reactions. Precious few react to what they observe.

Returning to our sports analogy, many athletes keep their eye on the ball as they make contact and watch its flight, but very few maintain their concentration by following through to the next action of the ball. That instinctive reaction is the winning edge of champions. The ball in sports is but a single inanimate object, while audiences to presentations are multiple dynamic objects. The champion presenter instinctively follows the reaction of each member of the audience and promptly Adjusts the Content. These dynamic exchanges produce head nods.

Read the Reaction and Adjust Your Content are also very much like air traffic control in aviation. The controllers carefully monitor radar screens, observing the flight paths of every airplane in the area and adjusting their traffic flow for optimal safety and efficiency. Monitor every member of your audience as you present or speak. Read the Reaction of each person and Adjust Your Content for their optimal understanding and, ultimately, their approval.

The Mental Method is a simpler and far more effective way to reduce the fear of public speaking than meditation, visualization, shouting, jingling coins, small-diameter bats, swinging rubber tires, or neurofeedback electrodes. Getting head nods from your target audience member does it all for you.

Read the Reaction/Adjust Your Content

Marya McCabe of Microsoft Corporation discovered the value of interaction with an audience the hard way: by backing into it. Marya is a district sales and marketing manager with Microsoft's Northwest sales district. Although she has been with the company for 10 years, Marya presents only infrequently. Recently, however, she was asked to present an unproven marketing concept to several internal audiences, most of whom, as Marya was painfully aware, would be resistant to the new ideas. A long row to hoe, to say the least.

The first time Marya presented, her worst fears came true. As she unfolded her story, she could see her audience's resistance in their dubious facial expressions, narrowed eyes, and stiffening body language. Marya reacted the way any human being would react to stress. She went into full Fight-or-Flight mode, and her presentation fell apart. What Marya did not know at the time was that she had already taken the first step toward controlling her audience: she had *Read their Reaction*. But that was only half of the solution. She had yet to take the next step: *Adjust her Content*. That didn't happen until the next time she presented.

This time she came prepared. Whenever Marya saw someone look skeptical or react negatively, she offered counter evidence. The effect was immediate: She saw their skepticism subside and, in some cases, she even got head nods. As soon as she saw them, Marya regained her composure and delivered her new concept with confidence and poise.

For her third audience, Marya took her interaction to the next level: She evoked the head nods proactively. Not only did she address the skepticism as it occurred, she also preempted her objectors by arriving with a set of negative questions that she posed rhetorically, and then provided her own answers. Each answer produced head nods, and each time she saw the nods, she settled down. Soon Marya came to expect the head nods. As she put it, "It gave me an opportunity to address what was controversial and support my story."

Marya had tapped into the full power of interaction: evoking the head nods with planned responses, as well as on the fly: *Reading the Reactions* of her audience and *Adjusting her Content*, live, and in real time.

Do as Marya did. You will soon discover that, as you become proficient in this powerful new technique, the positive energies of each interactive exchange will multiply and compound as you move around the room—first, arithmetically as you move from person to person; then, geometrically as the group dynamics gain momentum. The involuntary empathy radiates throughout the audience like ripples on a lake, creating almost irresistible waves of positive perception— about you.

The Dynamic Circle

Read the Reaction/Adjust Your Content complete the circuit of a chain reaction that can be viewed as a dynamic circle, shown in Figure 6.3.

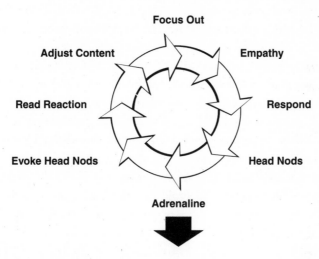

Figure 6.3 The Dynamic Circle

This dynamic circle begins with the snap of your mind from yourself to just one person in your audience. *Focus out*, away from yourself by thinking "you" and saying "you." This will stimulate empathy in the one "you" that you are addressing. That person will *respond* involuntarily with *head nods*. When you see the head nods, your *adrenaline flow* will diminish. You can *evoke more head nods* by continuing to Read the Reactions and Adjust Your Content. The complete circuit re-creates the conversational mode.

The power of this circuit was validated scientifically by Lawrence Steinman, MD, professor of Neurological Sciences, Neurology, and Pediatrics at Stanford University, who has twice been awarded a Javits Neuroscience Award by the U.S. Congress and the National Institutes for Health. Dr. Steinman is also the co-founder and a member of the board of directors of Bayhill Therapeutics, a company focused on the treatment of autoimmune diseases. He participated in a Power Presentations program in anticipation of Bayhill's IPO road show. At the culmination of the delivery skills session, the good doctor observed:

The Mental Method of Presenting controls the stress of public speaking because it taps into the basic principles of neurophysiology. Speaking before a group causes the release of adrenaline. This key neurochemical produces Fight-or-Flight behavior, which diminishes a speaker's effectiveness. But when a speaker connects with the audience and senses their responsiveness, the adrenaline flow and therefore the stress level recede. Then, when an audience observes a speaker's ease and confidence, remarkably, the listener experiences feelings of confidence and becomes more receptive to the speaker's message. These synchronous and synergistic emotions occur in the listener via stimulation of the mirror neurons in the brain. Neurology and physiology combine to create a powerful two-way loop that bonds the speaker and the audience.

When *you* complete that loop, you will enter the presentation or speech equivalent of the athlete's *zone*. From that moment on, you will know that you are not just standing there, helplessly exposed, shooting blanks into a dark, yawning chasm in front of you. You will be inside the room with your audience, engaged in two-way interactions with them. You will control your fear of public speaking *and* your audience. You will control your own destiny. You will win.

Proof Points

The power of the Mental Method of Presenting comes in two brief, but telling examples.

In the Power Presentations program coaching sessions, we ask each participant to stand and deliver a short presentation to the other participants. Each person presents the same information four times and we videotape each iteration. Between iterations, we playback each video to provide an objective point of view, as well as a progression of the same skills you are learning here. The first recording occurs before any instruction, to establish a baseline.

In one session, a young woman who was an experienced presenter delivered her baseline iteration quite easily. She was very comfortable in front of her peers, and she presented with considerable poise and animation. Then, when she sat down to see the video playback, she realized that she had forgotten to bring her eyeglasses and had to squint at the screen.

As the day progressed, she learned about reading the reactions of her audience. When she got to her fourth and final iteration, she stood up in front of the camera and spoke to one person at a time, but this time, she squinted. She had *not* squinted earlier in the day when she was delivering the identical content to the identical group. Although she had been looking at her audience during her seemingly effective initial iteration, she had not been connecting with them. The Mental Method enabled an effective presenter to truly engage with her audience.

For a personal experience, let's turn back to the example in chapter 4 of a speech I gave at an investment banking conference and the video recording that followed. During the entire speech, I was able to present at maximum effectiveness because I was focused on the audience. As I delivered my words, I watched how the individual members of the audience received them. I looked for their head nods, smiles of recognition, or quizzical looks, and I adjusted my content to what I saw. Whenever I saw understanding, I moved on; whenever I saw puzzlement or doubt, I elaborated briefly. But during the video recording, when I was focused only on myself and my performance—and had not Verbalized my material—I stumbled repeatedly.

Learn from my experience: *Read the Reaction/Adjust Your Content. Get the head nods. Get the endgame of the Mental Method of Presenting.*

Delivering Your Message

Here we are about a quarter of the way into this book and we've only now come to the point at which conventional presentation skills advice begins: the physical expression of your presentation or speech with your body language and voice. Over the course of my many years as a coach, I have found that this is what most people refer to or expect when they seek consultation for their mission-critical pitches. More often than not, I have been asked to coach *only* the delivery skills. These inquiries usually start by stating, "My story is set, my slides are set; all I need is for you to tell me . . ." and then conclude with one or all of the following: ". . . what to do with my hands and arms," ". . . how to slow down," ". . . how to make me louder," ". . . how to be less stiff," ". . . how to be more expressive," and the most common, ". . . how to calm my nerves and settle down."

Clearly, there is a great demand for advice on the delivery skills, simply because they are difficult to execute.

I have steadfastly declined all such requests, for if I were to start coaching the body language and voice of a person who had not carefully prepared his or her content, who did not have a complete understanding of the effects the adrenaline rush, and whose focus was on how he or she was doing rather than how the audience was doing—the essentials of the Mental Method—all that any coaching would produce would be moonshine, accompanied by a flapping of arms and flapping of gums—*full of sound and fury, signifying nothing.*

Now that you are armed with the tools to implement the foundation, you are ready to learn how to implement the delivery, to provide a launch platform for your payload message, to *suit the action to the word.* Now is the time to answer those frequently asked questions. Now is the time to begin the learning process of your delivery skills, the subject of the next chapter.

Learn to Speak with Your Body Language

Suit the action to the word, the word to the action; with this special observance, that you o'erstep not the modesty of nature.
—William Shakespeare
Hamlet, Act III, Scene 2

The Four Stages of Learning

If you've ever taken up the study of a physical activity, such as a sport, you've gone through a process known as the *Four Stages of Learning*. The stages also hold true for the physical aspect of presenting or speaking before a group. Whenever you start the process of seeking to learn new physical skills, you inevitably go through four clearly defined stages.

Stage One: Unaware of what to do, you perform poorly and are *unconscious about your incompetence.*

Stage Two: The instructor tells you what you did wrong and you become *conscious about your incompetence.*

Stage Three: The instructor tells you what to do and you become *conscious about your competence.* But the first time you try to follow the instructor's advice it feels unnatural. Your Stage Three, then, is actually *self-consciousness about your competence.* So the instructor tells you to practice the new skill often. Repetition over time is central to learning *any* subject, *any* skill, be it mental *or* physical. If you stay with it long enough, you can get to . . .

Stage Four: You perform your skill without thinking about it; you are *unconscious about your competence.*

Are you at Stage Four with your sport of choice? Are you there with *any* sport? Have you ever been there? It *is* possible, but it cannot happen overnight. You cannot go from beginner to expert easily and quickly. You cannot improve without going through *all* four stages. In fact, as you go through the stages you will most likely spend most of your time at Stage Three, *self-conscious competence.* You will undoubtedly feel discomfort when you attempt some of the new skills and exercises in this book.

The key for you to be able to make changes in yourself is to accept the discomfort. Accept that you will have to step outside your comfort zone—which brings us to a paradox.

Comfort Zone Paradox

When you are up in front of an audience and your adrenaline is flowing, driving you to flee or fight, to protect your vital organs, what *feels* comfortable is to cover your underbelly, to go into body wrap. Paradoxically, that behavior makes you *look* uncomfortable to your audience. If instead, you exhibit behavior that *looks* comfortable to your audience—opening your arms wide in welcome—you would *feel* exposed, open, vulnerable, and uncomfortable.

The paradox is expressed in the matrix in Figure 7.1, where the left side is the behavior side and the right side is the perception side. The

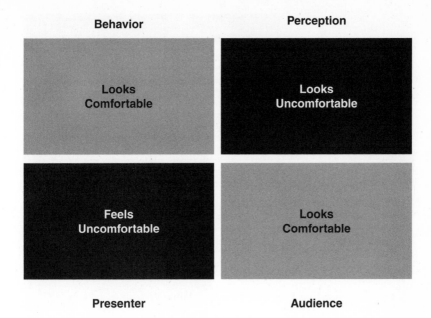

Figure 7.1 Comfort Zone Paradox

left side represents the presenter's point of view, the right side the audience's.

Taking a deeper look at the dynamics of Presenter Behavior/Audience Perception, let's recall the adrenaline-driven behavior described in chapter 3, shown in the form of the table in Figure 7.2.

Negative behavior, driven by the fear of public speaking and its attendant *instinctive* reaction, the Fight-or-Flight syndrome, creates negative perceptions in the audience. Once again, we have the same dichotomy: the very mechanism that enables us to survive in the wild makes us falter or fail in captivity—as presenters.

How do we change the behavior to create a positive perception? How do we make each of these elements work for us rather than against us? The key is to approach our challenge from the 35,000-foot view, and accept the paradox. If you can accept that there is a difference between the way it *feels* to you as a presenter and the way it *looks* to your

	Behavior	Perception
Eyes	Rapid Movement	Furtive
Features	Immobile	Fearful
Head	Sweeping	Harried
Hands & Arms	Body Wrap	Defensive
Stance	Rigid	Protective
Volume	Low	Weak
Inflection	Narrow	Monotonous
Tempo	Rapid	Rushed
Pattern	Steady	Data Dump
Unwords	Intrusive	Uncertain

Figure 7.2 Negative Behavior/Negative Perception

audience, please accept the acknowledged fact that the instructions you are about to learn are certain to make you *feel* uncomfortable.

When I coach my participants through these same exercises, I ask them to stand up in front of the room and gesture with their arms open wide. As soon as they do, I stop them and ask how it feels. Invariably, they reply: "Overdone!" "Strange!" "Exaggerated!" "Inappropriate!"

Undoubtedly, you will feel the same when you try the instructions. But, please, reserve judgment about how it *looks* to your audience.

You'll recall from the preface that before starting my own company, I worked as a hired hand for other companies, teaching delivery skills. I spent the better part of my business days asking the participants to perform new behavior. Because the new behavior *felt* uncomfortable to them, they inevitably resisted me. Nevertheless, I continued to browbeat or cajole them until they performed the new behavior. At the end of the day, they changed, but only slightly.

At the same time, they felt substantially worse. And so did I, for having inflicted such discomfort. The participants and I parted, each party feeling unhappy and unfulfilled. As soon as I discovered the paradox and started pointing out that the discomfort would diminish over time, my job got easier. More important, the participants made significant improvements. They were free to continue their ascent toward Stage Four, at their own pace, in their own time.

Repetition Over Time

Repetition over time will flatten out the paradox. Eventually, opening your arms will *feel* comfortable to you and continue to *look* comfortable to your audience. You will *look* poised, confident, and ready to take on the world. But keep in mind that it will take a considerable amount time for you to *feel* poised, confident, and ready to take on the world. You are not a racing car; you cannot go from zero knowledge to zero defects in 60 seconds flat. You cannot go from white belt to black belt in a day. It takes time.

Repetition over time reinforces habits. Whatever behavior you have been practicing until this point in your life is behavior you have been reinforcing. To develop new habits you need repetition. The hurdles are high, with different heights for different human beings, but highly worth vaulting.

It is the same as the skier who traverses the baby slopes many times until it becomes second nature and is then ready to move on to the advanced slopes. Repetition over time will move you from Stage Three to Stage Four, from *self-conscious competence to unconscious competence*.

Change

Joe Moglia is the chief executive officer of TD Ameritrade, a leading provider of self-directed investment services. Prior to entering the financial world, Joe was the defensive coordinator for the Dartmouth College football team; he also authored a book called *The Key to*

Winning Football: The Perimeter Attack Offense. Joe engaged my services to help craft Ameritrade's corporate presentation. During our sessions, Joe related to me as a fellow coach. He noted the similarities between the Mental Method of Presenting and his approach to football, and even to running a company:

Learning the new behavior requires going through discomfort. Because of the discomfort, people—and organizations—are resistant to change.

The key to effectuating change is to communicate to the individual— or the organization—that the discomfort is the price to pay to achieve the new results. If an athlete wants to excel, he or she will have to workout harder and longer. If an organization wants to improve its business, it will have to alter its tactics and perhaps even its structure. It will have to change.

To Joe's words, I add,

If a presenter wants to improve, that person will have to learn new behavior.

But I leave to Joe Moglia the last words on the importance of change:

The definition of idiocy is to continue to do the same things the same way and expect to achieve different results.

You can be certain that the changes you will be learning for your delivery skills will produce discomfort. *A tried-and-true sports adage tells us that new skills will feel worse before they feel better.* But keep your eye on the endgame; the journey through the discomfort will be well worth your effort. Master the change, master the techniques involved, and you'll become a master of the platform.

The Moment of Truth

Let's flash forward to your next mission-critical presentation or speech. The Moment of Truth has arrived. You hear the key decision maker in your audience say, "Okay, let's get started." Or you hear the master of ceremonies introduce you. Or you hear your name boom out over the public address system, intoned by the preceding presenter, or by the disembodied voice of an announcer known in the presentation trade as the "Voice of God." Now, however, having organized your content in advance and having Verbalized it to familiarity, you step up to the front of the room with much greater ease of mind.

You also remember what you read in chapter 6 and you throw that switch in your mind from "Uh-oh! They're all looking at me!" to Think "you." You focus on one specific "you" in your audience. You snap your concentration to that woman in the middle of the back of the room.

However, that woman is not aware of your *snap*. You must project your internal decision to her outwardly. You happen to possess your very own projection system to convey that mental decision: the 10 elements of adrenaline-driven behavior that you saw listed in the table in Figure 7.2.

Please note that all 10 fall into the two dynamics with the most impact upon audiences: the first five are the Visual and the last five are the Vocal. This chapter and the next two will show you how, through highly detailed, step-by-step instructions, to control each of the items in the table.

Of course, you cannot take the completed table or this book up to the front of the room with you, or you will appear to be using a crib sheet. Moreover, the list will be lengthy and that would give you far too much to do—and not to do. You would most likely start asking yourself, "What did the book say I should do with my hands and arms?" "How should I stand?" "How do I make eye contact?" "Am I loud enough?"

Before long, you would go into overload. In sports this is called *paralysis by analysis*. Not very sporting.

Instead, once the list of instructions is complete, I'll reduce all the granular details into shorthand: two easy-to-remember takeaways. I'll provide you with additional details in subsequent chapters, but I'll reduce them, too, into one more shorthand takeaway. That's a total of just three simple instructions; all you'll need to remember at The Moment of Truth.

Reduced Instructions

In fact, you already have the first of the three: the essence of the Mental Method, the shift outward: *Think you*. You won't be surprised that the other two instructions address the high-impact Visual and Vocal dynamics. You can view all three as a triangle, in Figure 7.3, with the base already filled in; the details of the vertical legs will follow.

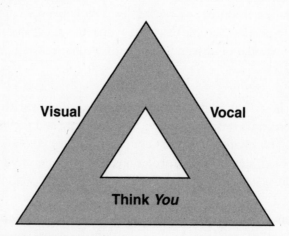

Figure 7.3   Reduced Instructions

The position of the Mental Method as the foundation of the triangle is intentional. A bit of perspective will illustrate why.

Earlier in this chapter, I described my work as a hired hand for other presentation skills firms offering delivery skills to business people. All I ever offered, however, were instructions about the two vertical legs of the triangle: the body language and the voice. I spent most of my days barking orders at people just like you, ordinary mortals, to: "Do this!" "Don't do that!" "Don't do this!" "Do that!" "Do it bigger, smaller, faster, slower, louder, softer, wider, narrower . . . !"

These instructions were appropriate during my days as a public affairs producer at CBS, where I was directing announcers, reporters, newscasters, and program hosts, all of whom were professional performers. Businesspeople, however, are professional only at their own job specialties, and when I treated them as performers, they balked.

"I'm not an actor!" "Hey, back off, Jerry!"

But I had a big bag of tricks and, when I deployed them, I got my business clients to do exactly what I asked them to do: "Bigger, smaller, faster, slower, louder, softer, wider, narrower . . ." At the end of the day, I had them pounding the lectern and bellowing their words.

Unfortunately, when they went out into the real world and tried to present, they were so busy thinking about themselves and trying to remember all the many commands I had given them, they got tied up in knots. Worse, they regressed to a point further back than where I had started with them. What's wrong with this picture? I was supposed to be providing services, *not* disservices.

As I moved into my own business, I realized that coaching delivery skills needed a different approach. The first challenge was to deal with the adrenaline rush by using the Mental Method as a foundation for the physical instructions. Next was to avoid analysis paralysis by *reducing* those instructions.

I chose a total of three because of what is known as the *rule of threes*, the widely held principle that three is the easiest amount to remember.

In addition, all three of the instructions you'll learn here are linked. The first, Think *you*, drives the other two: the body language and the voice. The third, which is the subject of a subsequent chapter, pulls through all the other instructions and loops back to the first. At the end, you will have another dynamic circle.

We begin with the Visual, the dynamic with the greatest impact upon audiences.

Visual Components

Eyes are at top of the list with good reason: They are the most important part of human communication. The power of the eyes has deep roots that go all the way back to the first moments of life. Marshall Klaus, MD, adjunct associate professor of Pediatrics at the University of California at San Francisco, is a distinguished neonatologist who has studied the behavior of mothers and their newborn infants. Among the primary dynamics Dr. Klaus explored is what he calls the *en face* position (parent and infant, face-to-face with their heads aligned in the same vertical plane) and, particularly, what he describes as "eye-to-eye contact."

Dr. Klaus noted, "The visual system provides one of the most powerful networks for the mediation of maternal attachment. The babies who received this kind of attention went into a state called 'quiet alert,' in which, rather than squirming and looking around as babies are apt to do, they remained focused on their mothers." So important is eye-to-eye contact, Dr. Klaus put a photograph of a mother holding her child *en face* on the cover of *Bonding*, one of his many authoritative books (Photograph 7.1).[1]

This early imprinting carries forward into the adult life of every human being. There are two common statements in Western culture: "I like that person; he looks me straight in the eye!" "I don't like that person; he's shifty-eyed!" In my programs, every time I begin to discuss the role of the eyes in interpersonal communication, I ask whether anyone in the group would ever hire someone who did not look them

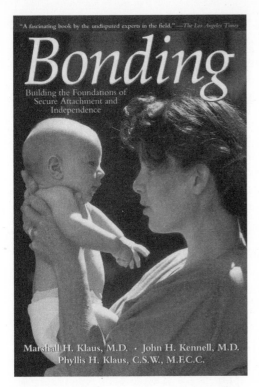

Photograph 7.1   Mother and Child in Eye-to-Eye Contact

straight in the eye during a job interview. Invariably, the answer is a resounding no!

The conventional wisdom then is to make eye contact.

Unfortunately the term *eye contact* is vague. Is it sweeping the room frantically looking for escape routes? No. Is it darting furtively from one person to the next? No.

Therefore, let's give it a more specific time frame and call it by a different name: Eye *Connect*. Every time you pick a person with whom to have a conversation, look at that person *at least* until you feel him or her look back at you. Feel the connection. Feel a *click*. Look that person straight in the eye. Establish *sincerity*.

Features were Ronald Reagan's strong suit and, as the Pulitzer Prize television critic quoted in chapter 1 wrote they produced millions of votes. Please revisit Video Frame 1.1 and notice Reagan's raised eyebrows, his crinkly eyes, and his warm smile. Emulate the Great Communicator: Be *expressive*. Raise your eyebrows, furrow your forehead, and smile. All these expressions stimulate positive responses to your message by projecting *enthusiasm*.

Your *head* is a superb vehicle for transporting your eyes from person to person, left to right and right to left in the horizontal plane; but a far more powerful movement is in the vertical plane: the *nod*. To demonstrate just how powerful, try this exercise: Turn to someone nearby and ask for a moment of his or her time. Ask the person *not* to nod back at you, then nod at the person. Try as he or she might, the person cannot resist, and *will* nod back at you. *Involuntary empathy, again.* The head nod indicates *agreement*.

This is not to suggest that you become a bobble-head doll. As you move from person to person in your audience, nod when you connect with a new person. Nod when you make your Eye *Connect*.

Nodding also builds on the value of the Mental Method. Now you have *two* ways you can evoke head nods:

- Read the Reaction/Adjust the Content.
- Nod your own head.

Your *posture* or stance should be *balanced*. Distribute your weight evenly on both your feet. The most stable figure in geometry is a triangle, with a wide base supporting a narrow top. Re-create the triangle with your whole body and the stability will make you appear *poised*. When your weight is not evenly distributed, you appear slack. What's worse, after a short while with your weight on one foot, your hip will grow tired and you will shift your weight to your other foot and become slack again.

When your body is balanced your mind also becomes balanced. Given the mind/body relationship, a balanced stance helps you focus your ideas more clearly.

Does this mean that you must rivet your feet in place and never move? Not at all; move all you want—if your move meets these two requirements:

- *Move purposefully to a destination*. Move to a person on one side of the room for a brief conversation, and then move to another person on the other side for another conversation. Move to the projection screen. Move to a demonstration table.

- *When you reach your destination, stop—balanced.* Conclude your move with your weight evenly distributed on both feet. Taken together with your purposeful movement, these two factors will keep you from wandering aimlessly back and forth, like a caged animal exhibiting the Flight Syndrome.

Hands and *arms* are the subject of the most frequently asked question in the presentation trade: "What *do* I do with my hands?" The answer is to do what most people do with their hands in conversation, *gesture to illustrate*.

In the interest of developing an individual style, I won't attempt to choreograph your gestures; nor should you. You may be a person who indicates big as tall, or you may be a person who indicates big as wide.

However, there is one gesture I *will* recommend, so it had better be a good one. Whenever you step up to the front of the room, you create a gap between you and your target audience. As a communicator, your job is to close the gap. Do it as the famous AT&T slogan recommends: *Reach out*.

The moment you *Reach out*, you replicate a *handshake*, one of the most universal symbols of human communication the world over. The handshake began as a gesture in the Middle Ages. The right hand was used to grip a sword, and when the hand was extended and empty in social exchange, it was an indication that a person was not armed. The open hand signaled, "I come in peace." Half a millennium of practice has embedded that same signal in our modern culture, and we are all conditioned to respond positively to the handshake. *Another example of involuntary empathy.*

To demonstrate just how involuntary, try this exercise: Turn to someone nearby and, without saying a word, suddenly extend your hand. Even if you have been in each other's presence for some time, the other person will invariably—and reflexively—extend his or her hand back.

While the distance between you and your audience in a presentation setting will keep them from extending their hands back to you, they will certainly feel engaged when you *Reach out* to them. The net effect is to create yet another means of interaction.

There are ample opportunities for you to *Reach out*. As part of the Mental Method of Presenting you will be thinking "you" and saying "you" extensively. Therefore, every time you say "you," accompany the word with your hand and arm extended. *Reach out*.

- "Let me show *you* . . ."
- "Why am I telling *you* this?"
- "Do *you* see what I mean?"
- And, let us not forget, WIIFY: "What's in it for *you*?"

The parallels between sports and presentations or speaking are uncanny. In tennis, golf, swimming, running, and soccer, *extension* is critical. You take full strokes in golf and tennis, rather than punch at the ball. You take full strokes in swimming, rather than dog-paddle. You take full strides in running, and you kick the soccer ball with full extension. During a recent soccer competition, a promotional television clip showed a player kicking a ball with his body extended in a full horizontal thrust, parallel to the ground. The video image froze him in midair to emphasize his athleticism and extension.

Do the same in your presentations and speeches: *Reach out* in full extension and unlock your elbow. The full extension replicates a firm handshake, the direct opposite of the socially undesirable weak handshake. Be sure that the full extension of your arm culminates with your palm open and *all* your fingers extended. If you have a tendency, as many presenters do, to point with your forefinger when gesturing, a simple mathematical equation will correct that: $3 + 1$. Unroll three fingers—your pinky, ring, and middle fingers—to join your forefinger in an open palm and a full handshake.

Despite all the many benefits of reaching out, you will find it *very* difficult to do. Your adrenaline will send counter signals to your arms, impelling them into protective body wrap. All of which brings us full circle to the Comfort Zone Paradox. As you saw in Figure 7.1:

- What feels uncomfortable to you looks comfortable to your audience.
- What feels comfortable to you looks uncomfortable to your audience.

When you are up in front of the room, exposed to an audience, and you try the new skill of reaching out, you will be fighting the instinctive impulse to wrap your body, and it will *feel* uncomfortable to you. But because you are replicating a friendly handshake to your audience, it will look comfortable to them.

Continue the full circle back around to the four stages of the learning process. *Reach out* is a new skill. The first few times you try it, you will be stuck at Stage Three, *self-conscious about your competence*. Over time, reaching out will feel better, and *every time* it will look better. The path to learning new skills is to accept that they will feel worse *before* they feel better.

Mix and match your reaching out and your gestures. Sometimes *Reach out* with your left hand, sometimes with your right hand, sometimes with both hands; sometimes point up as you say, "Our revenues are rising"; sometimes point down as you say, "We're reducing our costs"; sometimes thrust your arms wide open as you say, "This is a global opportunity"; sometimes tick your fingers as you enumerate, and sometimes do nothing. Let your hands fall to the *home base* position: at your side.

How will this feel? Undoubtedly, uncomfortable. Body wrap is essentially the adult version of the fetal position. It is a position you have been assuming since you were in the womb. You have repeated and, therefore, reinforced that position every time you stood exposed in front of an audience. This new home base position will feel exposed and vulnerable. How will it look? Comfortable. The Comfort Zone Paradox, again.

This is not to say that you should stand frozen as a soldier at attention. Think of your hands at your sides as a *touch-and-go* position. After you make a gesture with one hand, drop it to your side for an instant. Then make another gesture with the other hand and drop it for an instant. Reach out and then drop your hand for an instant. Enumerate with your fingers and then drop your hands for an instant. Every time you illustrate your talking points with your hands, drop them to your sides for punctuation.

The touch-and-go approach yields five benefits, each building upon the other:

1. When your hands drop to your sides, you will feel compelled to bring them back up quickly, to get them in front of your exposed underbelly. This movement, while somewhat comforting to you, will appear as animated to your audience and help illustrate your words.

2. When your hands come up from below your waist to gesture, they travel a greater distance than from the body wrap position, making that gesture more pronounced. If you say, "This is a very large opportunity," and your elbows are pressed against your sides, your hands will swing out in a very short arc, like a seal's flippers. Football coaches criticize players who do not extend their arms fully by calling them *alligator arms*. If instead your hands start from below your waist when you say, "This is a very large opportunity," they will traverse a greater space and express a larger opportunity.

3. When your hands and arms are in body wrap, your shoulders roll forward, inclining your head downward. When your hands

release from body wrap and fall to your sides, your shoulders roll backward and your head elevates, making you appear poised.

4. When one or both of your arms fall naturally to your sides, they put a visual period on your gesture—and words—as a punctuation mark.

5. The final benefit of dropping your hands and arms to your sides has the biggest payoff. When either arm comes back up from below your waist to *Reach out*, the movement will elevate your chest. Your arm acts as a handle on a water pump, and the action will contract your lungs, forcing your breath up and out, animating your voice.

Vocal Components

Because of this bellows effect, there is no need whatsoever for you to think of your voice production. In fact, if you were to try to speak louder, you would strain your vocal cords; if you were to try to speak lower, you would feel as if you were whispering; if you were to try to emphasize certain key words, you would feel as if you were acting. Reaching out from home base replaces all of these forced, performance-based efforts. *Reaching out **animates** the full range of your vocal production: both volume and inflection.* Reaching out connects all of your Visual components with your Vocal components and with your Verbal as well, because the pump effect on your lungs adds *variety* and *punctuation* to your content.

If you were to stop right here and stand up to try the preceding instructions, you would start furrowing your eyebrows, nodding your head, and flapping your arms all at the same time, and you would go into complete overload. Instead, we can distill all the preceding instructions into a short, easy-to-remember takeaway. But first, please note that all these instructions share one least common denominator: Each of them is qualitative, and *not* quantitative.

Qualitative versus Quantitative

As a coach, I never say, "Bigger, smaller, faster, slower, louder, softer, wider, narrower . . ." Those words are performance commands, and neither you, nor any presenter or speaker is a performer. Each of the instructions describes the *quality* of your engagement with the one person with whom you are having a conversation:

- Your *eyes* hold until they *connect*.
- Your *features* reflect your *enthusiasm*.
- Your *head* nods to create involuntary *agreement*.
- Your *balanced posture* appears *poised*.
- Your *hand* and *arm reaching out* replicates a *handshake*.
- Your *voice* conveys your message with *conviction* and *punctuation*.

The Chain Action

The preceding list of bullets can also be viewed as one continuous thread, a series of dynamic interconnections linking one instruction to another. To demonstrate, please try this exercise:

- Step up to the front of the room and *pick one person*—let's say the woman in the middle of the back of the room that you chose at the beginning of this chapter.
- *Think* about that woman. What does she know and need to know in order to respond favorably to your message?
- Eye *Connect* with the woman, and as you do, *Reach out* to her. As your hand extends, your body will follow. As you lean forward, your head will dip into a *head nod*, which will cause the woman to nod back to you *involuntarily*. In order to maintain Eye *Connect* with her, you will have to look up through your eyebrows, causing them to rise, making your features *expressive*.

Therefore, when you Eye *Connect* and *Reach out* in one continuous motion, you animate *all* your Visual dynamics. That same motion, extending your arm out from your chest, also compresses your lungs and animates your *voice*. Thus, the two brief *linked* actions, Eye *Connect* and *Reach out*, generate an extended chain action that animates all your Visual *as well as* all your Vocal components.

The big bonus of this chain is that Eye *Connect* animates your features without your having to think about it. Eye *Connect* activates a magic equation: *Engagement equals expressiveness*. Its antithesis, rapid eye movement, *precludes* expressiveness. Expressiveness is what got Ronald Reagan those millions of votes.

Of the many instructions in the chain above, three are pivotal:

- Eye *Connect*
- *Reach out*
- Animation

You can view the three as an equation:

Eye *Connect* + *Reach out* = Animation (as in Photograph 7.2)

(Photo by Rich Hall)

Photograph 7.2   Eye *Connect* + Reach Out = Animation

The same equation brings into force Sir Isaac Newton's Third Law of Motion: *Every action has an equal and opposite reaction.* As you reach your arm forward, you will feel as if you're about to fall over but your body won't let that happen. Your torso will produce an equal and opposite reaction and find its center of gravity. You will settle back and *stabilize your stance.*

This stabilization, in turn, will further help improve your Vocal production: It provides a solid launching platform for your voice. Opera singers are trained to plant their feet to add thrust to their voices.

I've reduced the detailed instructions considerably, but there's still too much for you to remember. The final distillation is to a simple three-letter acronym, ERA, for:

- **E**ye *Connect*
- **R**each *out*
- **A**nimation

ERA is the delivery system that lifts your story, your payload, into orbit. ERA brings the Visual, Vocal, and Verbal dynamics together as one force. As you move from person to person in your audience, ERA each person.

With ERA and Think *you*, you have two of the total of three instructions that encompass all the instructions thus far. The third involves the Vocal, but you now know that ERA serves to pump two of the five Vocal components, volume and inflection. The other three, Tempo, Pattern, and Unwords are *Cadence*, the subject of chapter 8.

As an example of the power of ERA, let's look back to 1991 and then come forward to today. During the first Gulf War, U.S. Marine General Richard Neal, the daily briefing officer of the Desert Storm campaign, appeared on worldwide television from the media room in Riyadh, Saudi Arabia, almost every day for the 43 days of the war.

Today, hardly anybody would recognize General Neal. During that same period, General H. Norman Schwarzkopf appeared in the same venue only about half a dozen times, and yet today he is as recognizable a celebrity as a nightly network news anchor.

Granted, General Schwarzkopf was the commander and General Neal was the daily briefing officer, but it was their widely differing delivery styles that created these widely different public perceptions. During his sessions, General Neal almost always presented with his back ramrod-straight and his arms in body wrap (Video Frame 7.1). General Schwarzkopf was the direct opposite. (Video Frame 7.2)

Video Frame 7.1   General Richard Neal

Note

To see these live video clips of Generals Neal and Schwarzkopf with commentary, please visit www.powerltd.com/tpp and use the pass code you saw in the introduction.

Video Frame 7.2   General H. Norman Schwarzkopf

When "Stormin' Norman"—as he came to be known—fielded reporters' questions, he often rested one elbow comfortably on the lectern, and casually crossed his ankles. While his weight was off-center, he looked anything but slack. It all had to do with his wide-openness. With his other arm hanging loosely at his side, he had no body wrap. The intrepid general appeared ready to take on all comers. One reporter came at him:

Can I ask you two questions? First, did you think that this would turn out . . . . I realize a great deal of strategy and planning went into it . . .

As General Schwarzkopf thrust his head forward to listen, he furrowed his eyebrows and locked his eyes on the reporter's; all this, and the general was not even speaking!

. . . but did you think that this would turn out to be such an easy cakewalk as it seems; and, secondly, what are your impressions of Saddam Hussein as a military strategist?

As he began his reply, General Schwarzkopf stood up straight, smiled, and let go a slight "Ha!" telegraphing what his impressions of Saddam Hussein would be. He looked straight back at the reporter and said:

First of all, if we thought it would have been such an easy fight, we definitely would not have stocked 60 days' worth of supplies in these log bases. So as I've told you all for a very, very long time, it is very, very important for a military commander never to assume away the capabilities of his enemy, and when you are facing an enemy that is over 500,000 strong and has a reputation that they have been fighting for over eight years, being combat-hardened veterans, had the number of tanks and the type of equipment they have, you normally don't assume anything.

Now General Schwarzkopf went back to the side of the lectern and propped his elbow on the edge again.

As far as Saddam Hussein being a great military strategist . . .

The general began enumerating his speaking points on the fingers of his left hand.

. . . he is neither a strategist, nor is he schooled in the operational art, nor is he a tactician, nor is he a general, nor is he a soldier. Other than that he is a great military man.[2]

The strong verbal content of the last sentence—the punch line— was the payload, and it was launched into orbit by General

Schwarzkopf's delivery system: the mockery in his voice and the visual emphasis of his body language. His *eyes* were like laser beams; as he enumerated, he *reached out* his left hand. The result was *animation* of all his Visual and Vocal dynamics. ERA (Video Frame 7.3.).

Video Frame 7.3   General H. Norman Schwarzkopf

General Schwarzkopf had it easy. He delivered his messages powerfully in a winning cause; but a powerful delivery can also reverse a potential losing cause, as evidenced by the most famous such example in American political history.

The Kennedy-Nixon Debate

In the U.S. presidential election of 1960, Richard M. Nixon, the sitting vice president, was a virtual incumbent candidate. Massachusetts Senator John F. Kennedy, at the age of 43, the youngest candidate ever, was of questionable maturity. Kennedy was also the second Roman Catholic to run for the office. The first, Al Smith, the governor of New York, had lost his bid 32 years earlier because of his religion. Catholicism was not yet considered mainstream in the early days of the twentieth century.

These factors combined to make Nixon the leader in the public opinion polls. He held a slight edge over Kennedy for that entire summer. Then, on September 26 of that year, the two men met in Chicago for the first-ever televised debate between presidential candidates. Kennedy was the first to speak.

In the election of 1860, Abraham Lincoln said the question was whether this nation could exist half slave or half free. In the election of 1960 and with the world around us, the question is whether the world will exist half slave or half free. Whether it will move in the direction of freedom, in the direction of the road that we are taking, or whether it will move in the direction of slavery.

Kennedy spoke his words straight into the camera (and, therefore, to the audience.) Looking the electorate right in the eye, he appeared confident and sincere as he continued:

I think it will depend in great measure upon what we do here in the United States. In 1933, Franklin Roosevelt said in his inaugural that this generation of Americans has a rendezvous with destiny.

Kennedy's stance was rock-solid, his weight evenly distributed on both feet, his shoulders level. His left hand rested lightly on the lectern. His right hand, while not reaching out in full extension (as you would do well to do), nonetheless moved animatedly (Video Frame 7.4).

Video Frame 7.4   John Kennedy Debating Richard Nixon

Note

To see this live video clip of the Kennedy-Nixon debate with commentary, please visit www.powerltd.com/tpp and use the pass code you saw in the introduction.

As Kennedy punched his right hand vigorously, the pumping action animated his voice and inflected his key words (italics are mine to indicate Kennedy's vocal emphasis).

I think our *generation of Americans has the same* rendezvous. *The question now is: Can* freedom be maintained *under the most severe attack it has ever known? I think it* can be, *and I think in the* final analysis *it depends upon* what we do here. *I think it is time* America *started moving again.*

Eyes, posture, gestures, voice: All the Visual and Vocal dynamics worked in unison to convey Kennedy's message. He looked and sounded stable, composed, poised, assured, and brimming with conviction. All these adjectives are synonymous with *presidential*.

Richard Nixon presented a very different image (Video Frame 7.5).

Video Frame 7.5   Richard Nixon Debating John Kennedy

Nixon's weight was on his right hip. As he slouched to one side, his right shoulder drooped. Both his hands clutched the lectern with white-knuckle intensity. He looked tense, defensive, and fretful. None of these adjectives is synonymous with *presidential*. A more appropriate description would be the *deer in the headlights*.

With no pump action of his arms, his flattened voice made his words drone on without emphasis.

> *Let us take hospitals. We find that more of them have been built in this administration than in the previous administration. The same is true of highways. Let's put it in terms that all of us can understand.*

At that point, Nixon's right hip got tired and he shifted his weight to his left hip, and came down unbalanced on his other side. During the shift, his hands never released his death grip on the lectern. He appeared even less presidential.

A short while later in the debate, Kennedy spoke about Nixon.

> *Mr. Nixon comes out of the Republican Party . . .*

The television director of the debate was Don Hewitt, the man who was to become the driving force behind CBS's *60 Minutes*. Because Kennedy was talking about Nixon, Hewitt appropriately decided that he should show Nixon. In television, this is known as a cutaway or reaction shot. This being the first-ever televised debate, Nixon was not aware that when he was not speaking he could still be seen on camera. Kennedy continued,

> *. . . he was nominated by it. And it is a fact that through most of these last 25 years the Republican leadership has opposed federal aid for education, medical care for the aged, development of the Tennessee Valley, development of our natural resources . . .*

As the camera suddenly cut from a shot of Kennedy speaking to a close-up of Nixon listening, Nixon's eyes darted from side to side, and then off into space. His rapid eye movements continued as Kennedy voice continued.

I think Mr. Nixon is an effective leader of his party; I hope he would grant me the same. The question before us is which point of view and which party do we want to lead the United States.

In 1950, during the election campaign for U.S. senator from California, Nixon ran against Helen Gahagan Douglas. It was a nasty campaign, filled with mud-slinging and name-calling. Mrs. Douglas labeled Nixon "Tricky Dicky." Ten years later, during Nixon's first solo run for national office, his furtive eye movements in the debate with Kennedy revived the label.

A footnote to history provides perspective on Nixon's eye movement. The clock in the Chicago television studio was situated over Nixon's left shoulder. Therefore, whenever Nixon spoke, Kennedy could look at him and see the clock without having to shift his own eyes. As a result, in the reaction shots of Kennedy, his eyes barely moved, and he looked focused and intent. Alternatively, when Kennedy spoke, Nixon had to flit his eyes away from Kennedy to see the clock. The close-ups of Nixon showed only his face, and not the clock, making his eye movements appear furtive.

When Kennedy concluded his observations about Nixon, one of the panel of reporters, Stuart Novins of CBS, who was sitting several feet away from the candidates' lecterns, asked,

Mr. Nixon would you like to comment on that statement?

Nixon's eyes darted away from Kennedy to find Novins, and then they flitted off into space, appearing furtive, as he replied:

I have no comment.

Later, Novins asked:

Would you tell us please specifically what major proposals you have made in the last eight years that have been adopted by the administration?

During Nixon's response, his stance remained slack. Then the mind/body factor kicked in: his imbalance threw off his concentration and he stumbled over his words.

It would be rather difficult to cover them in eight—er—two and a half minutes. I would suggest that these proposals could be mentioned. First, after each of my foreign trips I have made recommendations that have been adopted. For example after my first trip abr—er—abroad I strongly recommended that we increase our exchange programs particularly as they related to exchange of leaders in the labor field and in the information field.

Nixon appeared halting and uncertain.

In the final segment of the debate, as Kennedy delivered his closing statement, the director, Hewitt, continued to insert reaction shots of Nixon, and Nixon's eyes continued to dart. Kennedy's eyes continued to be steady.

If you feel that everything that is being done now is satisfactory, that the relative power, prestige, and strength of the United States is increasing in relation to that of the communists, that we are gaining more security, that we are achieving everything as a nation that we should achieve, that we are achieving a better life for our citizens and a greater strength, then I agree and I think you should vote for Mr. Nixon. But, if you feel that we have to move again in the '60s, that

---

> the function of the president is to set before the people the unfinished business of our society as Franklin Roosevelt did in the '30s, the agenda for our people, what we must do as a society to meet our needs in this country to protect our security and help the cause of freedom.[3]

Two days after the debate, the Gallup organization took another poll. In a striking reversal of fortune, Kennedy took the lead and held on to it until his victory. Those poll respondents who had watched on television thought Kennedy had won, while those who had listened on the radio thought Nixon had won.[4]

The Visual dominated the Vocal and the Verbal.

Several other factors impacted the candidates' appearances and, therefore, the outcome of the debate.

- In the days leading up to the debate, although Nixon was fighting an infection, he continued to campaign vigorously. He arrived at the television studio exhausted and underweight, his clothing hanging loosely. Kennedy had rested for three days prior to the debate, even taking the time to sit in the sun.
- When Nixon arrived at the studio, he banged his knee on the car door, which probably caused him to favor that knee and shift his weight. Kennedy, with his chronic back pain, wore a corset to support himself.
- Nixon's aides applied a slapdash coat of a product called "Lazy Shave" to his characteristically heavy beard, making him look pasty. Lazy Shave was not porous, which caused Nixon to perspire through the coating, making him look nervous. Kennedy used a light coat of professional makeup, which was porous.
- Nixon wore a light suit that blended with the light studio backdrop and made him look washed out. Kennedy wore a dark suit that contrasted with the background and made him stand out.

All of the above, however, were purely external factors. The primary influence on the audience perception was the presenter behavior. Nixon, himself, would later admit: "I had concentrated too much on substance and not enough on appearance."[5]

Don Hewitt agreed. In his autobiography, he recalled, "What I particularly remember about that night was that Kennedy took it a lot more seriously than Nixon did."[6]

From that moment on, no candidate for any office, national or local, would ever again treat television debates trivially, or consider appearance and style subordinate to substance. The Kennedy-Nixon debate was the seminal event that changed the face of political campaigning forever. No longer could or would any candidate succeed without having or acquiring powerful delivery skills. Ronald Reagan's twin presidential victories in the eighties, Bill Clinton's twin presidential victories in the nineties, and Barack Obama's Run for the Roses and presidential victory in the twenty-first century are all essentially extensions of John F. Kennedy's gold-standard public-speaking style.

Whether you run for president or for your local town council—or not—whatever Run for the Roses you make, whether for financing, partnership, customer acquisition, or project approval, your delivery style will be viewed in light of the elevated standards we see in our public leaders. While you may not attain gold-standard status as a speaker, you can aspire to be the best that you can be.

All you need to do is ERA—Eye Connect, Reach out, and Animate— the same behavior you use in conversation. So, whenever you step up to the front of the room to present or speak, have a conversation with each person in the audience. But keep in mind that conversations are not one-way streets. Use the Mental Method of Presenting. Read the Reaction of each person you address and be prepared to Adjust your Content. Keep your eye on the ball; watch it land and be prepared to return the serve.

Earlier in this chapter I defined the length of Eye *Connect* as *at least* until the person with whom you're conversing looks back at you—until you feel the *click*. Now I'll become more specific, by defining the duration of each of your engagements, which relates to the *cadence* of your conversation, the subject of the next chapter.

CHAPTER

8

Control Your Cadence

No word was ever as effective as a rightly timed pause.
                                        —Mark Twain

Cadence in speech is the equivalent of rhythm in music. Music needs a beat and speech needs a beat, a metric. For our speech metric, we turn to our three presentation dynamics and focus now on the Verbal, or the content. In text, the written form of the Verbal, that metric is a sentence. In documents, words are grouped in sentences.

Spoken language, however, is different. When we speak, we don't form full sentences; we speak in incomplete or partial sentences. Turn to any newspaper or magazine article that contains a transcript of an interview and you will see how fragmentary spoken language appears when written. Spoken ideas are formed in fractions, interrupted by ellipses, or ramble on as protracted thoughts that veer off into discontinuity. If you try to follow the context of a transcribed interview, you often have to back up and reread a given passage.

The audience for your presentation or speech does not have that luxury. If they lose track of what you are saying, they will fall behind and will have to work to catch up with you—a prescription for failure. Instead, if you speak in a clear and coherent cadence, it will make it easy for your audience to follow you.

Speak in a rhythm that meters the progression of your verbal presentation. Speak with a beat. In speech, that metric is a subdivision of a sentence, the irreducible unit of spoken language: the *phrase*.

Some phrases are very long and convoluted, containing many, many words. Some phrases are shorter, consisting of fewer words. Others are shorter. Others shorter still. Shortest. Therefore, a phrase can be multiple words, two words, one word.

Regardless of the number of words, every phrase shares a common characteristic with every other phrase: Every phrase is a complete entity. Every phrase is an integer. Every phrase has a beginning and an end. Every phrase parses your content into whole bytes. The phrase gives your cadence *logic*.

To make the phrase the basic rhythm of your spoken cadence, you must also consider what separates one phrase from another. The Vocal equivalent of a written punctuation mark is *a pause*.

Here's how it all works together in a presentation or speech: When you step up to the front of the room, pick one person in your audience, the one with whom you're going to have a conversation. Then:

- Deliver one phrase to that person.
- Pause.
- Move to another person and deliver one phrase to that person.
- Pause.
- Move to another person and deliver one phrase to that person.
- Pause.
- Continue around the room, delivering one phrase to one person at a time.
- Pause between each phrase and each person.

Phrase and Pause

You will soon come to discover that this Phrase and Pause skill is a most powerful tool; but every tool can cut both ways. For example, if I were to look you straight in the eye, and say: "The key to winning presentations is . . . " and then suddenly darted my eyes away as I finished the phrase, " . . . the Mental Method!" how would that feel? Not very good. It would feel abrupt at best and rude at worst.

Finish the phrase to the eyes of the person with whom you are engaged. Stay with him or her all the way to the end of, "The key to winning presentations is the Mental Method!" and *then* move your eyes to engage with a different person. Staying connected for a mere three additional words may seem insignificant, but the difference in impact is enormous. Try these two variations of the same phrase with someone you know. Even as an exercise, the difference will be palpable.

Now let's focus on the pause, the interval of time that occurs as you move from one person to another. Many events take place during that silence. Leading off the list, you can *think* of your next phrase; a significant benefit, because it helps to ease your mind. The silence also allows the audience member you have just addressed to *absorb* what you said; another significant benefit, because it gives that person time to reflect on your words. While those two benefits are very important, there is another, even more important—more important than the other two put together: you *breathe*.

The breath you take contains oxygen, which, in addition to extending your lifespan, relaxes you, and further counteracts the adrenaline rush.

As you take that breath, you cannot utter a word, you cannot make a sound. You cannot say, "um," the dreaded *un*word. Try it. Take a deep breath, and as you do, try to say "um." You cannot. Inhaled air cannot produce voice.

The dreaded *unword* is the universal anathema of presentations. Accumulated custom in the presentation trade has made the "um" a heinous sin. Speakers avoid saying "um" like the plague, and when they utter even one, they feel like failures.

Most approaches to eliminate *unwords* are based on negative conditioning such as, "Don't say 'um'!" Or, "Every time you say 'um' you have to pay a quarter!" Aversion therapy doesn't work for nail-biters or smokers and it doesn't work for presenters. Telling a perpetrator what *not* to do usually causes the perpetrator to do it more often. If you tell an agitated person to calm down, that person will very likely become more agitated. The adrenaline rush in presentations is a form of agitation. Telling a presenter not to say "um" will simply produce more "ums."

Try the positive approach in presentations. Simply pause and breathe. That is the *only* way to eliminate *unwords*.

The breath you take during the pause has still another benefit: It fills your lungs with air, providing more fuel for your vocal pump, and *more animation in your voice*.

Therefore, the pause gives you five benefits, all for just coming to a complete stop.

- Presenter thinks.
- Audience absorbs.
- Presenter breathes.
- *Unwords* vanish.
- Voice animates.

The first two benefits above have subbenefits related to the rapidly shrinking nature of the world and the equally rapid global expansion of many businesses. Because many presenters today speak English as a second language, the pause that provides them time to think also gives them time to *translate* internally the words from their native language. Many of my business clients speak English as a second language very well. However, regardless of whether their first language is Chinese, Japanese, Hindi, Tamil, Spanish, French, Italian, or Hebrew, every time they pause, their comfort level improves immediately.

Moreover, because those same second-language presenters are likely to speak English with an accent, the pause also gives their audiences processing time to *comprehend* the unfamiliar pronunciations. I recently worked with a Frenchman who used the word "ontairpreez" during his presentation. But I didn't understand the word until he paused and allowed me to figure out that he had said "enterprise." Later on in his presentation, when he said "ze 'oull onsheelahdah," I understood that he was saying "the whole enchilada" even before he paused.

Of course, those English speakers who are fluent enough to present in a second language will reap the same corollary benefits to themselves and their audiences.

The pause provides even more primary benefits. For one, it *reduces sensory overload*. During the pause, as you move from away from the person to whom you finished your phrase, your eyes sweep across an unpopulated space. In that space you may see a coffee cup, a stack of paper, a mobile phone, a water glass, another coffee cup, a pair of eyeglasses, a computer, and then, finally, the next person. All those images are bits and bytes of data that your eyes take in. Your optic nerves instantly transmit those images to your brain, and your brain processes all of that inbound sensory data reflexively. If, at the same time, your brain is also attempting to process outbound sensory data—your ideas and words—and you speak, the two energy paths collide and you hit the wall. The overload makes your mind go blank. *Tilt!*

Images on computer monitors and television sets are created by electronic signals that scan across the surfaces of their screens repeatedly, refreshing their images. If your eyes move from person to person rapidly, taking in even more data, your brain has to work even harder to process each of the many new inbound images rushing into your eyes and your brain.

All this sensory processing produces a cascade effect: Your brain transmits your overload to your adrenal gland, which triggers the Fight-or-Flight Syndrome, which produces negative behavior, which creates a negative perception in your audience, which is manifested by their restlessness, which tells you that your presentation is faltering, and which stimulates even more adrenaline flow. The vicious cycle becomes a vortex and the cascade becomes a raging flood.

If, instead, you are completely silent as you make that trip across the unpopulated space, your brain has to process only the inbound data. In one fell swoop, the pause shuts down the cascade and reduces sensory overload.

The benefits continue. As you finish your phrase and start your pause, you will *punctuate the phrase succinctly* rather than ramble on and on. You can also *Read the Reaction* of the person who has just received the phrase, and if he or she frowns, or nods, or smiles, or looks dubious, you can *Adjust your Content*, implementing the Mental Method. All of which creates *a positive perception* of you with your audience.

The final benefit of the pause is major: you *control your tempo*. In chapter 7, I shared with you that, as a coach, I never ask people to speak faster or slower, because one cannot speak faster or slower. I was born and raised in New York City and cannot speak slowly. If I were to try to slow down, it would sound as . . . if . . . my . . . battery . . . were . . . running . . . down. Instead, Ispeakveryquicklywithineach-phrase. Then I pause. Then Ispeakveryquicklywithinthenextphrase. Then I pause. Therefore, I don't slow down. I *control the tempo*.

Now you have five more benefits of the pause.

- Reduce sensory overload.
- Punctuate.

- Read the Reaction/Adjust the Content.
- Earn a positive perception.
- Control your tempo.

That's a total of 10 benefits, all for the price of doing absolutely nothing!

The importance of the pause in speech is comparable to the role of the rest in music; the rests are as integral to a composition as are the played notes. Notes and rests in music correspond to phrases and pauses in speech; each member of each pair contributes equally to the overall cadence.

Think of Frank Sinatra and Ella Fitzgerald, two great popular singers who were acclaimed as much for their interpretive phraseology as for their vocal quality. Mr. Sinatra and Ms. Fitzgerald often held some of their pauses as long as their notes. Amanda Carr, a contemporary jazz singer, defines the pause in music as " . . . the element of space that shapes phrasing as much as the notes." And Dizzy Gillespie, the great jazz trumpeter, gave us his own inimitable definition of the pause: "It's taken me most of my life to know which notes *not* to play."[1]

While all 10 benefits of the pause in speech are important, one rises above all the rest: your *audience absorbs*. The pause gives your audience time during the silence to think about the phrase you have just completed. The more time they have the more they can reflect on your idea. Imagine your audience reflecting on each of your phrases as if they were savoring a spoonful of the rarest and most expensive Beluga caviar. Don't force them to wolf down such valuable matter. Don't be guilty of the often-stated charge, "Listening to him/her is like trying to take a sip of water from a gushing fire hose!"

Now you have chapter and verse for the Phrase and Pause skill, but you cannot lug this book and all this detail up to the front of the room with you. Once again, it's time to reduce all the instructions into an easy takeaway.

Speak Only to Eyes

Think about that for a moment. Speak only when you are in Eye *Connect* with one person. There are no eyes between people, so be silent during your pause. The converse of Speak Only to Eyes is: Do *not* speak during the traverse. But that is aversion therapy again. Speak Only to Eyes tells you what *to* do, rather than what *not* to do.

The London Underground (subway) system provides an analogous instruction: When trains enter stations with curved platforms and come to a stop, the curve creates a small space between the car and the platform, a minor hazard for boarding passengers. With typical British courtesy and understatement, a placard advises riders, "Mind the gap." Mind the gap between sets of eyes in your audience, move across the gap in silence. Speak Only to Eyes.

You can think of Speak Only to Eyes as single shot rifle, in contrast to a machine gun. The sharpshooter fires one bullet at a time; the machine gunner fires continuously, wasting many bullets. Deliver one phrase to one person at a time and don't waste your valuable phrases into the air, to no person at all. And don't lose the 10 benefits of the pause by speaking while in the gap.

* * *

There are two apocryphal notions floating around the presentation trade that correspond to Phrase and Pause. The first is that the presenter should "finish the thought." But this vague instruction is likely to produce a thought that contains multiple phrases all fired at one audience member, depriving that person of the time to absorb any of the phrases, and depriving the presenter of the time to think. The other eight benefits of every pause are lost, too.

The other apocryphal notion is about timing, and it recommends that the duration of a phrase should be three or four seconds; and a companion notion that the duration of the pause should be a second or two between phrases. Either of these notions would require the presenter to count while speaking or while thinking, either of which would immediately produce further sensory overload.

Speak Only to Eyes obviates the need for counting. *The pause takes as long as it takes for your eyes to move from the eyes of one person to the eyes of another person.*

* * *

Let's turn back to sports for another analogy. In tennis you can either hit the ball on the run or planted. The latter is preferable because both feet planted solidly provide a stable platform from which to launch your next shot.

The analogy is applicable to interpersonal communication. Let's say you were to deliver one complete phrase to one person: "The key to winning presentations is the Mental Method." But, then, if you were to start your next phrase *on the run* before you reached the next person, "And the key to the Mental Method is . . . " you would appear rushed to that person. You, too, would feel rushed, and that would activate the cascade effect.

Moreover, by starting the next phrase on the run, you would be speaking into what was known in World War I trench warfare as "no-man's land." You would address no one, you would appear impersonal. Mind the gap.

Instead, wait until you make Eye *Connect* with the next person *before* you start your next phrase; wait to speak until you land; wait until you plant *both* your eyes on *both* the eyes of that next person. Then, from your stable platform, launch your next shot. Say, "The key to the Mental Method is to Think *you*." Just as it was with staying with a person's eyes until you finish a phrase before you move, the delay until you see *both* eyes of the next person before you speak is but a mere instant, but the difference in impact is enormous. *Speak Only to* **both** *Eyes.*

This simple instruction produces a string of important benefits, each triggering involuntary empathic reactions from your audience.

- *Instinct.* Both your eyes connecting with both the eyes of a person in your audience re-creates the early imprinting of the *en face* or eye-to-eye contact, of the mothers and babies in Dr. Marshall Klaus's study.

- *Head nods.* Your head will dip into a nod when you speak to both eyes, causing the person with whom you are connecting to nod back *involuntarily*. The mirror neurons at work.

- *Expressiveness.* To maintain Eye *Connect*, you will have to look up, causing your eyebrows to rise, animating your features. Please recall the magic equation from the previous chapter: *Engagement equals expressiveness.*

- *Sincerity.* When both your eyes are engaged with both the eyes of an audience member, you appear sincere. To create sincere images of people, portrait photographers and painters often pose their subjects with their irises, the colored circles, centered in their eyes, flanked by the whites of their eyeballs.

- *Logic.* You will deliver your content with a clear starting point.

- *Punctuation.* By Speaking Only to *both* Eyes you eliminate the first word in the phrase, "*And* the key to the Mental Method is . . . " This seemingly innocuous conjunction is, in its own way, an *unword* because the "and" that begins the subsequent phrase connects two disparate phrases. In doing so, the "and" not only makes each phrase more difficult for the audience to process, it also omits the pause and all of its 10 benefits. Eliminate the "and" makes each phrase distinct.

- *Pause.* When you Speak Only to *both* eyes, you control the entire duration of the pause: its beginning, middle, and end.

To paraphrase the words of General Israel Putnam in the Revolutionary War, "Don't *speak* until you see the whites of their eyes."

Complete the Arc

While Speak Only to Eyes defines the specific length of the pause, we also need to define the specific length of the phrase. At the beginning of this chapter, I described the phrase as a complete unit with a variable number of words, and illustrated them as follows:

Some phrases are very long and convoluted, containing many, many words. Some phrases are shorter, consisting of fewer words. Others are shorter. Others shorter still. Shortest.

Regardless of the length, however, each phrase has a logical unity that cannot be broken. Using the same example, if I were to look you straight in the eye and say, "The key to winning . . . " and then, with my voice hanging in midair, leave you, it would sound foreshortened. Even if I were to pause all the way across the gap and wait until I landed on both of another person's eyes to finish the phrase, " . . . presentations is the Mental Method," it would sound incomplete. The full meaning of the phrase would be fractured.

Instead, stay with one person for the entire logic of the phrase— regardless of its length—and then drop your voice. Stay with that one person for the full trajectory of meaning. As with the pause, the length of each unit is measured logically rather than numerically. Dropping your voice at the end of every phrase is called *Complete the Arc.*

Stay in Eye *Connect* all the way through the full phrase, "The key to winning presentations is the Mental Method," and then drop your voice at the end.

If you do not drop your voice at the end of your phrase, if you let it hang in midair, you convert your statement into a question. A question indicates uncertainty, and uncertainty appears tentative; the complete opposite of the confidence that every presenter aspires to exhibit. This is another example of the effectiveness matrix shown in Figure 2.2 where, in the case of the upper left quadrant, a high story is driven down by low delivery.

At the far other end of the spectrum, teenagers tend to speak with rising inflection at the ends of their phrases, making their words—and their personas—sound immature. This pattern is known as "Valley Girl talk." *Complete the Arc.*

Film and video editing offer a vivid example of the importance of Completing the Arc. We've all seen the television news clip in which a subject, a senator for instance, is saying, "I think that that's a great idea . . . " then, with the senator's rising voice suspended in midair, the clip abruptly switches to a shot of a reporter, who comments on the senator's statement. The rise in the senator's voice at the switch is known among film and video editors as an *upcut* because it makes a viewer wonder whether there was something more to the statement. Did the senator go on to say, "but . . . " and then continue on to disparage the idea? Did the editor alter the meaning of the senator's statement? A negative perception.

Let's turn again to music for another parallel with speech cadence. Musical phrases are constructed as irreducible integers whose logic must be resolved. Think of the famous theme from Ludwig van Beethoven's Fifth Symphony and its familiar pattern of three short notes followed by a long one: *Bam-Bam-Bam BAM*. The final *BAM* creates resolution of the musical phrase. If you were to hear only *Bam-Bam-Bam . . .* , it would sound incomplete.

From the sublime of Beethoven to the ridiculous: "Shave and a haircut, two bits." This universally familiar rhythmic snippet is often expressed without words, as a knock on a door composed of a long note followed by four short notes followed by two long ones: *BAM-Bam-Bam-Bam-bam, BAM BAM.*

Try this exercise: When you are next with a group of companions or colleagues around a conference or restaurant table, out of the blue, rap your knuckles on the tabletop: *BAM-Bam-Bam-Bam-bam* . . . then stop short. The odds are that one or two of your companions, without any prompting, will rap their knuckles on the tabletop: *BAM BAM*—Completing the Arc.

This instinctive impulse to resolve the logic of a musical phrase transcends cultural borders. Dr. Krzysztof Izdebski, the chairman of the Pacific Voice & Speech Foundation, invited me to present the Complete the Arc concept at the organization's annual conference. The attendees were voice and speech scientists from all over the world: Japan, Russia, Scandinavia, and Western Europe. After Dr. Izdebski's introduction, I stepped onto the stage and, without uttering a word, rapped my knuckles on the lectern: *BAM-Bam-Bam-Bam-bam*, then stopped short. Without a word, several people in the audience rapped their knuckles on whatever hard surface was nearby—their seats, their armrests, their laptops, or their brief-cases—*BAM BAM!*

After the conference, Dr. Izdebski published *Emotions in the Human Voice*, a series of scientific volumes that captured many of the concepts presented during the sessions. Here's how Claude Steinberg, one of the presenters at the conference, described Complete the Arc in scholarly terms:

[I]nformation-dense monologue is at great risk of confusing and alienating audiences, of producing the emotion of revulsion in place of whatever the speaker hoped to elicit, unless it presents one idea at a time, each idea separated by a phrase-final fall in pitch followed by a breath-long pause. [2]

The convergence of music and speech is vividly demonstrated in a DVD called *The Unanswered Question*, featuring Leonard Bernstein, the legendary conductor and composer. The DVD is a record of a series of lectures Bernstein delivered at Harvard University in which he explored the interdisciplinary relationship between music and speech. Bernstein illustrated the relationship in both his content and his own cadence. He used long, looping sentences with many complex clauses to express his erudite concepts, yet in every one of them, he Completed the Arc. Listening to Bernstein speak words is like listening to him conduct music.

One other instance of music and speech convergence comes from another conductor. In February 2008, Lorin Maazel, the resident conductor of the New York Philharmonic led his orchestra on a tour of North Korea in an effort to build a cultural bridge between the countries where conventional diplomacy had failed.

Mr. Maazel decided to precede his concert by attempting to greet his hosts in their language, Korean. His solution, one he had used successfully in Japan, was to "write a musical score to complement a more conventional phonetic transliteration of his remarks in Korean . . . his Pyongyang score would cue him on cadence and rhythm and all the other elements of speech."[3]

Despite the maestro's fluency in seven other languages, the complexity of Korean presented too stiff a challenge and he abandoned the idea, but his instincts about cadence and rhythm to convey meaning were on the right track and are applicable even when speaking in one's own native language.

An illustration of the importance of Completing the Arc in speech comes from President George W. Bush. In the election campaign of 2000, Bush, then governor of Texas, debated Vice President Al Gore three times. Their last debate, on October 17, 2000, at Washington University in St. Louis, was conducted in the town hall format in which citizens had the opportunity to question the candidates directly.

> **Note**
>
> To see the live video clip of the Bush/Gore debate with commentary, please visit www.powerltd.com/tpp and use the pass code you saw in the introduction.

One came from a young woman, who asked, "How will your tax proposals affect me as a middle-class, 34-year-old single person with no dependents?"

Governor Bush answered,

Uh . . . you're going to get tax relief under my plan . . .

As he spoke the last three words, his voice hung in midair, without dropping. He did not close his mouth or take a breath.

Because he did not Complete the Arc, he rolled directly into his next phrase, accelerating his words.

. . . you're not going to be targeted in or targeted out . . . everybody who pays taxes is going to get tax relief.

With barely a pause for a very short breath, he continued to roll his words, jamming the last two phrases together, his cadence now starting to slide into a ramble.

If you take care of an elderly in your home . . .

"If you take care of an elderly in your home!" A few moments earlier, the young woman had said that she has no dependents. By not pausing, Mr. Bush lost thinking time and lost track of her question. The ramble took him off topic.

. . . you're going to get the personal exemption increase. I think also what you need to think about is not the immediate, but what about Medicare?

"Medicare!" The young woman was 34 years old, almost double her entire life span away from Medicare eligibility. Mr. Bush's ramble took him further out on a limb, making him appear evasive and off-message. No pause, no separation, no beginning or end, no completion of the arc.

You get a plan that will include prescription drugs, a plan that will give you options. Now, I-I-I hope people understand . . .

Now he began to sputter.

. . . that Medicare today is . . . is . . . is important . . .

His sputtering continued. Instead of pausing to recover, he blurted into his next phrase.

But it doesn't keep up with the new medicines. If you're a Medicare person on Medicare . . .

"If you're a Medicare person, on Medicare": his ramble now produced a redundancy in reverse.

. . . you don't get the new procedures . . . you're stuck in a time warp, in many ways. So it will be a modern Medicare system that trusts you to make a variety of options for you.

More jammed phrases, more inadequate breaths, more run-on rambling, no pausing, no thinking, and no completion of the arc, all accumulating to drive his fragmented thought patterns to veer sharply into yet another topic:

You're going to live in a peaceful world . . .

And then for good measure:

It'll be a world of peace . . .[4]

"A peaceful world . . . a world of peace": another redundancy in reverse.

To add insult to injury, at that very moment, the television camera cut away from Governor Bush to the young woman who was shaking her head dubiously, with a most dissatisfied look on her face.

Negative behavior produces negative perceptions.

In chapter 5, you saw that President Bush was able to overcome his chronic difficulty with the English language by making improvements in his delivery style over the course of just a few months. One of the most important factors he changed was his cadence. The evidence came in his watershed speech following the September 11, 2001 attacks on New York City and Washington, DC. Nine days after those tragic events, he addressed a joint session of Congress and the nation:

Tonight we are a country awakened to danger . . .

He dropped his voice when he said "danger." He closed his mouth and paused, Completing the Arc.

. . . and called to defend freedom.

He dropped his voice when he said "freedom." He closed his mouth and paused, Completing the Arc.

Our grief has turned to anger and anger to resolution.

He dropped his voice when he said "resolution." Then he closed his mouth and paused—a very long pause.

Whether we bring our enemies to justice or bring justice to our enemies, justice will be done.[5]

Every man and woman in that entire chamber stood in a rousing ovation: positive behavior, positive perception (Video Frame 8.1).

Video Frame 8.1 George W. Bush, Post-9/11 Speech

Note

To see the live video clip of George W. Bush's speech with commentary, please visit www.powerltd.com/tpp and use the pass code you saw in the introduction. The clip continues on to include the video clip of the Bush-Putin press conference.

In the photograph, please note the two vertical black rods immediately in front of the president's podium; they are the supports for the transparent Plexiglas teleprompter screens on which the text of his speech scrolled. Arguably, you might say that comparing an extemporaneous presidential debate to a scripted speech is comparing apples to oranges, and it is—somewhat. Presidential debates are rehearsed and practiced virtually to the point of scripting, and that debate was no exception. To compare apples directly to apples then, let me illustrate the improvement in George W. Bush's cadence in the extemporaneous setting of a press conference.

On November 13, 2001, following a meeting at the White House with Vladimir Putin, the president of the Russian Federation, President Bush held a joint press conference.

Note

The live video clip of the Bush/Putin press conference with commentary is combined with the video of the Bush Post-9/11 speech from Video Frame 8.1.

A reporter asked Mr. Bush:

You mentioned you had discussions on the ABM Treaty. What progress are you making? And are you convinced you won't have to withdraw from the treaty now?

Mr. Bush replied:

Well, I'm convinced that the treaty is outdated and we need to move beyond it. And we're having discussions along those lines.

He dropped his voice when he said "lines," Completing the Arc.

We had good discussions today; we had good discussions in Shanghai; we had good discussions in Slovenia; and we'll have good discussions in Crawford.

He dropped his voice when he said "today," "Shanghai," "Slovenia," and "Crawford," Completing the Arc each time.

This is obviously a subject that's got a lot of ramifications to it. I clearly heard what the president has had to say, and his view of the ABM Treaty; he's heard what I've had to say. And we'll continue working it.

Working without a script, but comfortable in his new brief-phrase, short-arc cadence, Mr. Bush appeared at ease and confident all at once.

But my position is, is that it is a piece of paper that's codified a relationship that no longer exists . . .

His voice dropped when he said "no longer exists," Completing the Arc.

. . . codified a hateful relationship. And now we've got a friendly relationship.

His voice dropped each time he said "relationship," Completing the Arc each time. Coasting on a wave of confidence, he concluded his answer on the upbeat.

And I think we need to have a new strategic framework that reflects the new relationship, based upon trust and cooperation. But we'll continue to work it.[6]

President Bush went on applying the short-arc cadence in both his scripted speeches and extemporaneous appearances throughout his first term and into his second. Using brief phrases, he developed a crisp pace by dropping his voice, closing his mouth, pausing frequently, and controlling his rhythm. This newfound skill served him well, making him sound more confident and assured.

As a spot-check, let's flash forward to the opening words of his final State of the Union address on January 28, 2008.

Madam Speaker, Vice President Cheney, members of Congress, distinguished guests, and fellow citizens:

Seven years have passed since I first stood before you at this rostrum. In that time, our country has been tested in ways none of us could have imagined. We have faced hard decisions about peace and war, rising competition in the world economy, and the health and welfare of our citizens. These issues call for vigorous debate, and I think it's fair to say we've answered that call.[7]

Notice the many commas, and periods in the transcript. Mr. Bush turned each of these written punctuation marks into Vocal phrases and pauses, making the delivery of his Verbal message very effective.

Develop your own effective cadence by employing the key dynamics of Phrase and Pause, all of which can be summarized as follows:

- You define the Phrase when you *Complete the Arc.*
- You define the Pause when you *Speak Only to Eyes.*

Combine these steps with the Mental Method of Presenting. Consider your presentation or speech as a series of person-to-person engagements in which you have individual conversations, and *make every conversation a* **complete** *conversation.*

As succinct and as simple as these instructions may seem, the fear of public speaking is going make them very difficult to execute. Adrenaline-driven time warp makes every pause feel like an eternity. I was not born with the ability to Phrase and Pause. In fact, as a native of New York City, I was raised with the firm conviction that to pause is to surrender. It was difficult for me, as I'm sure it will be for you—or for any person in front of any audience—to apply this skill. It requires practice to develop fluency. In my own learning process, I developed two techniques that I offer to you.

Two Practice Techniques

The first is to go into an unoccupied conference room and have your person-to-person conversations with the empty chairs, as if there were people sitting in them. This will help you to pace your movement around the room. As you move from one chair to another, be sure to do so in random sequence, as you should when you are in front of a real audience. If you move in predictable, shooting-gallery fashion, your audience will quickly pick up the pattern and lose attention during the gaps. If you move randomly, they will stay attentive.

The second approach is to go into your room or office alone with a digital or tape recorder and record yourself presenting or just speaking on the telephone. Then play back the recording and listen to your cadence from an objective viewpoint. Listen for whether you parse the data into complete arcs or whether you ramble. Think of the times you've listened to a recorded message on your voicemail by someone who rambles:

"Hi! I'm just calling to confirm our lunch today and I was wondering where you think we should eat because I know that you like Chinese food but MSG doesn't agree with me and you

(continued)

---

can't have Italian food because you're on a low-carb diet and neither of us wants Mexican food because it's too spicy but salads are really bland and boring so I was wondering what you think . . . "

At which point you are most likely ready to hit the Delete key on your telephone keypad. Don't inflict a ramble on your audience, and risk them wanting to delete you.

You will be able to find your own arcs when you Verbalize into the recorder and listen to your cadence. By focusing on your voice, you eliminate the need to think about your Visual components, and concentrate only on your Vocal cadence and your Verbal content. Record several iterations of the same passage and listen to whether you do or do not Complete the Arc by dropping your voice at the end of each phrase. As you repeat the exercise you will gain proficiency and find your own optimal speech pattern. Of course, the ultimate benefit is that it will be your own *natural* pattern.

This audio-only rehearsal method serves to prepare you for two other important communication modes. One has been with us for over a century, and the other for only about a decade. In both, your audience has only your voice and your content to perceive, and not the more personal elements of your eyes, features, and body language. The first is the telephone conversation, and the second is the presentation delivered over the Internet with only your voice and slides. The second, virtual, form of presenting, provided by Microsoft LiveMeeting and Cisco Systems WebEx, among others, is rapidly growing in popularity. With both the telephone and the Internet, your voice is the prime conveyor of your content, and you cannot sound like the unbroken, flat-line voicemail message example above. It would be like sending a document without punctuation. Give your audiences Vocal punctuation for your Verbal content. Deliver your important message with a crystal-clear cadence. Complete the Arc.

The First 10 Seconds

Now let's move forward to your next mission-critical presentation or speech. The moment you stand up in front of that room the adrenaline will start coursing through your body. It will cause your eyes to sweep the room in search of escape routes. You will not be able to hold back that sweep. You will not be capable of thinking about pausing. You will barely be able to think of what to say. Your eyes will go into motion, searching for the exits.

Go with it. Let the sweep happen. Sweep long enough for your eyes to determine which escape route you will take—should the need arise. Let your eyes take in the entire room; but make the sweep work for you rather than against you. Accompany your continuous eye movement by speaking to the entire group, and be gracious about it: "Good morning. Welcome. I appreciate the opportunity to speak with all of you." These simple amenities will make your rapid eye movement appear sincere rather than frantic. Be sure to make your amenities brief. No Academy Award acceptance speeches here.

Golfers walk the course before their game to get the lay of the land. They do this to see where the sand traps and the woods are located. Take a lesson from the golfers; let your eyes walk your presentation course with your sweep. (It's also a good idea to walk your presentation course with your feet. I do. For every new presentation environment, whether for a small group program session or a large group keynote venue, I arrive early and walk around the room to check the audience sightlines. Then, I go to the front of the room to check my own sightlines. When the actual presentation begins, I begin by sweeping the room with my eyes during my amenities. I do this every time, even though I present almost every business day of the week.)

Once you have swept the room with your welcoming remarks, stop. Turn to one new person, set on both of that person's eyes, and get ready to speak the first phrase of your presentation. Have that first phrase clear in your mind.*

This first person to receive your first phrase should be a considerable distance away from the last person at the end of your sweep. If you sweep your eyes to the right, stop, and move to a new person on the left side of the room; if you sweep to the left, stop, and move to a new person on the right side of the room.

There are two very good reasons for this wide swing. One is to give you a fuller pause to think—thinking is always a good idea. The other is to make that first phrase to that first person very explicit. Think of it as stepping up to the baseline in tennis. You don't serve as soon as you get there. You plant your feet, you look across the net at your opponent, you take a breath, you may even bounce the ball; all to be in a stable position to deliver a hard, fast serve. Your first phrase to the first person is your serve. Make it an ace.

At the end of that first phrase, pause and turn to another person to deliver another phrase. Continue to move around the entire room in that same pattern: one person, one phrase, and then pause. Establish your cadence, and stay in your cadence.

The San Francisco 49ers professional football team originated a formula for their game plan that other teams adopted: Script the first 10 plays of every contest for a strong start. Once again, we have a parallel between sports and presenting. Script the first 10 phrases of your presentation or speech. The quotation marks around script indicate that you should develop the general ideas of those phrases rather than memorize them. Once you've done that, Verbalize the phrases until you become familiar with them. Don't carve them in stone; Verbalize them

---

* Make the first phrase of your presentation the first phrase of your Opening Gambit, a rhetorical technique to capture your audience's attention immediately, covered in detail in my book *Presenting to Win*.

until you find your flow. Think of the first 10 phrases as expansions of one Roman column. Establish the rhythm for your entire presentation in the first 10 phrases.

Give your presentation or speech a strong start by sweeping your eyes as you speak your brief welcome to discharge your adrenaline rush, and then follow the welcome by delivering your presentation in a clear, crisp Phrase and Pause cadence. Keep in mind: *You never have a second chance to make a first impression.*

Large Groups

The same tactic of the eye sweep followed by a clear, crisp first phrase delivered to one person is applicable to all groups, small and large. Start strong and continue strong. As you move around the room, continue to speak to one person for one phrase. That said, there are some special considerations for audiences of more than 100, known as *Big Tent* presentations.

- *Depth of Field.* Have you ever sat in the audience at the back of a large room and had the presenter turn toward you and say, "You, sir, or "You, ma'am"? Uncertain as to exactly where the presenter was looking, you most likely looked around and said, "Who, me?" At a certain distance it is difficult to see the presenter's eyes. This is the depth-of-field factor, and it works in favor of the presenter. When you deliver a phrase to the back of a large room, several people feel as if you are addressing them directly.
- *Blinding lights.* When you are in a really big tent (an audience in the hundreds) and are illuminated by blinding lights, you cannot Speak Only to Eyes, for you cannot see any eyes. Instead, move on your phrases. Deliver a phrase to a spot in the dark. Move to another spot in the dark and deliver another phrase. Find a pair of eyes at the edge of the light and deliver a phrase to that person. Then move to another spot in the dark and deliver a phrase. Be sure to make your moves in random sequence.

To summarize, Phrase and Pause produces positive behavior that will create a positive perception about your cadence.

- *Tempo* by phrases (versus fast or slow) is *well-paced*.
- *Pattern* of complete phrases has logic that creates *clarity*.
- *Unwords* replaced by pauses sound *natural*.

Phrase and Pause also culminates the changes in of all the items you first saw in the Negative Behavior/Negative Perception table in Figure 7.2, now with Positive Behavior/Positive Perception in the table in Figure 8.1.

	Behavior	Perception
Eyes	Connect	Sincere
Features	Expressive	Enthusiasm
Head	Nods	Agreement
Hands & Arms	Reach Out	Handshake
Stance	Balanced	Poised
Volume	Projected	Conviction
Inflection	Varied	Punctuation
Tempo	Phrases	Well-paced
Pattern	Varied	Clarity
*Un*words	Pauses	Natural

Figure 8.1 Positive Behavior/Positive Perception

Phrase and Pause is also the last of our three reduced instructions. It serves to fill in the vertical legs of the triangle, first shown as Figure 7.3 and now completed in Figure 8.2.

These reduced instructions can be reduced even further to a simple equation:

$$1 : 1 : 1$$

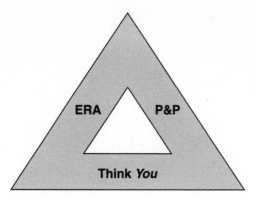

Figure 8.2 Three Reduced Instructions

One-to-one *for* one: Person-to-person for one phrase. This simple formula is essentially a summary of the entire book. Always speak one-to-one, regardless of the size of the audience. Make your presentations or speeches *complete* person-to-person conversations.

The triangle that represents the three reduced instructions can also be viewed as a circle of interlocking arrows, shown in Figure 8.3, which links all the instructions in a continuous chain.

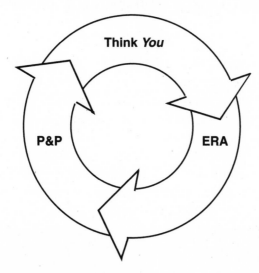

Figure 8.3 Three Linked Instructions

Think *you* establishes your *concentration* on one person in your audience; ERA puts you into a *conversation* with that person; and Phrase and Pause determines the duration of that conversation with a logical *cadence*.

Once you have completed your conversation with one person, move to another person and start around the circle again. This pattern will carry you around the room in a series of person-to-person conversations. Remember that conversations are not one-way streets. Read the Reaction/Adjust the Content as you move from person to person.

Adrenaline causes you to do the opposite of the instructions in the circle in Figure 8.3. Adrenaline drives you to:

- Think "I" (Most presenters ask themselves, "How am I doing?")
- Feel exaggerated when you Reach out (the Comfort Zone Paradox)
- Perceive a pause as an eternity (Time Warp)

Override the adrenaline. The first step, Think *you*, will reduce your adrenaline flow. Then engage in a conversation with one person, that specific *you*, and maintain that engagement for a complete unit of logic.

In the ultimate amalgamation, Phrase and Pause brings together all the elements of presentation dynamics: Deliver a logical unit of your Verbal content to one person with your Vocal components, and engage with that person with your Visual components by looking him or her straight in the eye while extending your hand.

As simplified and as natural as I have tried to make these skills for you, each of you will ultimately evolve a delivery style incorporating various degrees of any of the components. Just as every human being has a unique fingerprint, every human being develops a unique delivery style—even the masters of the game, as you will see in the next chapter.

CHAPTER 9

Masters of the Game

*[T]ell them to go out there with all they got and win just one for the
Gipper.*

—Knute Rockne, All American
First National Pictures, 1940
screenplay by Robert Buckner

The Great Communicator

The first example in this book of the power of the Visual and Vocal
dynamics was Ronald Reagan. Now that we've spent multiple chapters
analyzing the elements of positive presenter behavior, let's take another look at the Great Communicator to see what makes him so
effective. An excellent illustration is found in his delivery of his final
State of the Union message.

On January 25, 1988, in the House Chamber of the U.S. Capitol
Building, Ronald Reagan stood poised on the historic dais, looking out
at the sea of faces in a joint session of Congress. He spoke *with*—not
at—the men and women of the Senate and House of Representatives.
As he headed down the homestretch of the speech, the warm tone of
his voice expressed the reflective human-interest words of the text.

Note

To see this live video clip from Ronald Reagan's final State of the Union, please visit www.powerltd.com/tpp and use the pass code you saw in the introduction. And as you watch this video, shut your eyes for a moment and listen to his long phrases; notice how he Completes his Arcs.

But my thoughts tonight go beyond this. And I hope you'll let me end this evening with a personal reflection. You know, the world could never be quite the same again after Jacob Shallus, a trustworthy and dependable clerk of the Pennsylvania General Assembly, took his pen and engrossed those words about representative government in the Preamble of our Constitution.

After completing that long, graceful arc, he paused for a beat, and then resumed.

And in a quiet but final way, the course of human events was forever altered when, on a ridge overlooking the Emmitsburg Pike in an obscure Pennsylvania town called Gettysburg, Lincoln spoke of our duty to government of and by the people and never letting it perish from the Earth.

The vast, packed chamber watched and listened in hushed awe, drawn in by the hypnotic long, looping rhythms of his cadence.

In the next section of the speech, his words elevated from the personal to more lofty, universal, ideas, expressed in even longer arcs. Ronald Reagan rode each arc like a stately ship rolling on the high seas, its stout hull carrying it majestically over the waves.

At the start of this decade, I suggested that we lived in equally momentous times . . . that it is up to us now to decide whether our form of government would endure and whether history still had a place of greatness for a quiet, pleasant, greening land called America. Not everything has been made perfect in seven years . . . nor will it be made perfect in seven times 70 years . . . but before us, this year and beyond, are great prospects for the cause of peace and world freedom.

It means, too, that the young Americans I spoke of seven years ago, as well as those who might be coming along the Virginia or Maryland shores this night and seeing for the first time the lights of this capital city, the lights that cast their glow on our great halls of government and the monuments to the memory of our great men . . . it means those young Americans will find a city of hope in a land that is free.

As the speech reached its climax, Reagan displayed all the dynamics the Pulitzer Prize-winning television critic described in chapter 1: ". . . his physical presence begins to eclipse his words . . . when you begin watching more and hearing less . . . feeling more and thinking less. Look and mood completely take over. That presence on TV: just the sight of him cocking his head with his sincere grin and lopsided hair, is still worth a thousand words and millions of votes."

We can be proud that for them and for us as those lights along the Potomac are still seen this night . . . signaling, as they have for nearly two centuries and as we pray God they always will, that another generation of Americans has protected and passed on lovingly this place called America, this shining city on a hill, this government of, by, and for the people. Thank you and God bless you.[1]

Throughout the speech, Reagan spoke every word with bell-like clarity, articulated to perfection. At age 77, however, his once-resonant radio voice had become thin and wispy, in marked contrast to the voice of another man who stood at the very same spot on that historic dais 47 years earlier.

The Great Orators

Less than three weeks after the Japanese attack on Pearl Harbor, British Prime Minister Winston Churchill came to the United States to express his nation's support for its ally. On December 26, 1941, he spoke to a joint session of Congress from the venue of presidential State of the Union addresses.

Throughout his 30-minute speech, Sir Winston's characteristic stentorian tones and aristocratic eloquence rang throughout the chamber. As he drew to a close, his imposing figure stood in quiet dignity, his arms resting at his sides.

Still I avow my hope and faith, sure and inviolate, that in the days to come, the British and American people will, for their own safety, and for the good of all . . .

Then, in an expansive gesture, his arms rose grandly and reached out to the packed chamber (Video Frame 9.1).

Note

To see live video clips of Winston Churchill, John F. Kennedy, Martin Luther King, and Billy Graham with commentary, please visit www.powerltd.com/tpp and use the pass code you saw in the introduction. The sequence includes Video Frames 9.1, 9.2, 9.3 and 5.3.

Video Frame 9.1   Sir Winston Churchill, Speaking to a Joint Session of Congress in 1941

Churchill's closing words rang with determination.

. . . walk together in majesty, in justice, and in peace.[2]

When he concluded, he lifted one hand and raised two fingers in his trademark "V" for victory sign. It brought the audience to its feet, in thunderous applause.

Now compare President Reagan's presentation style to that of President John F. Kennedy, as seen in his classic inaugural address, delivered on the steps of the very same Capitol building in Washington, DC. January 20, 1961 was a bitterly cold day with a chilling wind and a temperature of 22 degrees, but Kennedy took the oath of office without a hat or topcoat. He stood at the lectern with his shoulders thrust back and his head held high, and said:

> *I do not believe that any of us would exchange places with any other people or any other generation.*

At this point he extended his right arm fully and, as his powerful voice bellowed the crisp words in his Boston accent, his arm beat the phrases like a concert master of a marching band.

> *The energy, the faith, the devotion which we bring to this endeavor will light our country and all who serve it. And the glow from that fire can truly light the world.*

Next he drew his right arm in closer to his side and beat the words with only his forearm.

> *And so, my fellow Americans . . .*

Now he extended his forefinger to emphasize his words.

> *. . . ask not . . .*

His forefinger continued to emphasize his words, tapping on the lectern.

> *. . . what your country can do for you . . .*

His forefinger came up again, extended for a moment, and then curled back under his thumb, forming the trademark gesture that Bill

Clinton would later emulate. Kennedy's hand punched the air, animating the point of his message (Video Frame 5.3).

. . . ask what you can do for your country.[3]

On August 28, 1963, just two and a half years later and two and a half miles across town, the Reverend Martin Luther King, Jr. stood on the steps of the Lincoln Memorial and delivered an equally classic speech. Following a civil rights march, Dr. King spoke before a crowd of 200,000 people.

He stretched out his arms and, in his rich, liturgical voice, intoned:

When we let freedom ring from every village and every hamlet, from every state and every city . . .

He dropped his voice and let his hands fall to the lectern.

. . . we will be able to speed up that day when all of God's children . . .

Both his arms came up again, his hands now clenched tightly.

. . . black men and white men, Jews and gentiles, Protestants and Catholics . . .

His arms dropped again, as did his voice, for just a moment. Then his voice began a crescendo.

. . . will be able to join hands and sing in the words of the old Negro spiritual:

His right hand alone began to rise, stretched out to the crowd (Video Frame 9.2).

Video Frame 9.2   Reverend Martin Luther King, Jr., Delivering His "I Have a Dream" Speech

Free at last!

His right hand continued to rise along with the crescendo of his voice.

Free at last!

Now, with his right hand pointing straight up to the heavens, his voice reached its pinnacle.

Thank God Almighty we are free at last![4]

Another man of the cloth who was as gifted an orator as Dr. King was Reverend Billy Graham. Richard Nixon once said to Graham, "When you went into the ministry, politics lost one of its potentially greatest practitioners."[5] Nixon was surely referring to Graham's power to mesmerize audiences.

That charisma was clearly evident in 1961 during Graham's England crusade at a packed stadium in Birmingham. Clad in a simple layman's dark suit, he stood proudly behind a lectern, his massive head held high. A full mane of blond hair framed his handsome features, and his rich voice pealed out his words as if they were emanating from the pipes of a colossal church organ.

There's something about coming out and standing quietly for a moment in front of a crowd . . .

He pumped his clenched hands up and down to emphasize his key words.

. . . that settles it and seals it.

Shooting his left forefinger heavenward, he intoned:

It testifies to heaven that you're not ashamed.

He dropped the hand, paused for a contemplative moment, then thrust out his right arm, pointing out to the furthest reaches of the stadium and said:

You say, "But it's so far from where I am back here," yes.

Now his left arm shot out and, once again, pointed heavenward.

But Jesus went to the cross for you.

Next he extended both arms up to the sky.

He hung openly in front of a crowd for you.

Then he extended both arms out to the crowd.

Certainly you can come a few feet for him, to give your life to him. You come, we're going to wait on you.

He clasped his hands reverently for a moment before extending his left arm (Video Frame 9.3).

Every head bowed while we wait.

Then Graham implored the crowd:

Just get up, right now, quickly. Hundreds of you, all over the place. Come.[6]

Video Frame 9.3   Reverend Billy Graham

Each of these world-famous orators used his hands and arms expressively. But not Ronald Reagan. In his farewell State of the Union address, and for most of his other speeches, Reagan did not use his hands and arms *at all.*

By the time he delivered that final annual speech, his hands had become arthritic and he kept them out of camera range. Moreover, State of the Union addresses are carefully scripted and run on a teleprompter, so Reagan used his hands to hold a backup hard copy of his speech (Video Frame 9.4).

Note

This Video Frame is at the conclusion of Ronald Reagan's final State of the Union address referenced at the beginning of this chapter.

Video Frame 9.4   Ronald Reagan, Flanked by Teleprompter Panels, Holding a Copy of His Final State of the Union Address

Therefore, all of Ronald Reagan's expressiveness occurred above his broad, solid shoulders, in his head and features. Those descriptive words of the Pulitzer Prize television critic captured it all: ". . . cocking his head with his sincere grin . . ."

This distinctive delivery style was not new to Ronald Reagan, and it did not come about as a result of the ravages of time or the fallibility of teleprompters. It emerged more than 30 years earlier, during a unique part of his film career. No, *not* his acting. Reagan's outstanding communication skills are often mistakenly attributed to his career as an actor when, in fact, even the kindest of critics did not praise his performances in his 54 films, most of them B-movies.

However, during the twilight period between the end of his acting days and the beginning of his political career as the governor of California, Reagan took on an assignment that was to crystallize his unique style. From 1954 to 1962, he was the host of an anthology series on CBS television called *General Electric Theater*. His job was to provide on-camera introductions and conclusions to short dramas.

Reagan's host segments were usually filmed at a different time from the productions of the screenplays. With Hollywood's customary logistical efficiency, Reagan often recorded several openings and closings at a time, in a bare studio, with only a camera and a production crew present. Yet he had to project his words and personality into the inert lens of a camera and through to audiences who would not see him for months, if not years, or even decades later. To be welcome in the living rooms of mid-twentieth-century America, Ronald Reagan had to present himself as one of the family, to be empathic, to be *conversational*.

He had developed this intimate quality even before he became a screen actor. In the early 1930s, he worked as a sports announcer at a radio station in Des Moines, Iowa. His job was to sit in a studio and, from a telegraph ticker tape, describe the play-by-play of Chicago Cubs' baseball games as if he were in the ballpark. Then and there, Ronald Reagan learned the art of projecting himself across time and space and, by extension, into the homes of his audiences.

By the time he got to Hollywood in the late 1930s, he had perfected his personable manner. It was undoubtedly reinforced by the role model of President Franklin D. Roosevelt, whose Fireside Chat radio broadcasts were captivating the nation at the time. Then, after nearly two decades and countless film and television roles as the All-American guy-next-door, Reagan's conversational style became his trademark.

One such 1954 episode of *GE Theater* is illustrative. A young, strapping Ronald Reagan, with the same lopsided—and color—hair as he had in his 1988 State of the Union, stood in front a bare wall of a movie studio, framed by stage lights. Attired in a smartly tailored tweed coat, sprouting a natty pocket kerchief, he propped his right arm casually on a stage light and let his left hand rest comfortably in his trouser pocket (Video Frame 9.5).

Video Frame 9.5   Ronald Reagan on General Electric Theater

Note

To see this live video clip from Ronald Reagan's GE Theater appearance with commentary, please visit www.powerltd.com/tpp and use the pass code you saw in the introduction.

He opened the episode with these words:

In a moment, in an answer to a great many requests, we'll present a film of a fine performance by James Dean in a General Electric Theater play.

His voice dropped on the word, "play," Completing the Arc.

It was a performance that helped attract nationwide attention to his talent, and we present it as one of the landmarks in his progress toward the great roles of his brief career.

His voice dropped on the words "brief career," Completing the Arc.

Those of us who worked with Jimmy Dean carry an image of his intense struggle for a goal beyond himself and, curiously enough, that's the story of the boy he portrays tonight.

He Completed the Arc and paused for a beat, then resumed.

Eddie Albert is the narrator, Natalie Wood the girl, in Sherwood Anderson's "I'm a Fool."[7]

It was all there: ". . . cocking his head with his sincere grin . . ." all the warmth and sincerity that was to go on to net him those "millions of votes," *and he never moved his hands and arms!*

A commercial DVD called "Ronald Reagan: The Great Communicator" contains many clips from more than 100 of his presidential appearances during the eight years of his presidency. In all the clips, he rarely used his hands and arms. Yet, in every clip, the Reagan charm comes shining through, expressed by that cocked head, sincere grin, lopsided hair, those twinkling eyes, that majestic cadence, and that silvery voice.

Conversation and Empathy

Contrast Ronald Reagan's conversational style to that of the four orators you saw earlier in this chapter. Winston Churchill, John F. Kennedy, Martin Luther King, and Billy Graham all used their hands and arms with dramatic gestures that approached choreography. All four had rich, resonant, nearly operatic voices. Moreover, the first two, Churchill and Kennedy, were national leaders who spoke from on high, down to their audiences, and asked them to come up to their lofty level. The latter two, King and Graham, were religious leaders who also spoke from on high, and asked their audiences to go up to a higher authority.

Ronald Reagan, on the other hand, spoke to his audiences at *their* level, as one of us. Churchill, Kennedy, King, and Graham forcefully projected their personas to the distant backs of their public rooms; Reagan gently projected his into private living rooms. It was the skill he had begun in radio and mastered during those eight years on *General Electric Theater*, radiating his personality to unseen strangers across a vast gulf of time and space; the skill that carried him from Iowa to Hollywood to Sacramento and, ultimately, to Washington.

The essence of Reagan's style was his uncanny ability to be completely at one with his audience in every setting, across every dimension, to make every person in every audience feel as if, "He's speaking to *me!*"

Being conversational begets positive empathy *involuntarily*. No other president ever achieved the approval ratings that Ronald Reagan did. He was the irresistible force that moved every object, every audience, every time.

You may not reach the heights that Ronald Reagan attained, but you can use his array of conversational skills as a role model and adapt them to your own delivery style. Emulate Ronald Reagan: Be yourself.

Barack Obama emulated Ronald Reagan. While Obama's rousing delivery of his keynote speech at the 2004 Democratic National Convention in Boston's giant Fleet Center (as discussed in chapter 2) mirrored the impassioned rhetoric of John F. Kennedy and Martin Luther King, his speaking style in smaller venues—campaign speeches, fund-raisers, town hall meetings, television debates, media inter-views—where he can more readily connect with his audiences, is much closer to Reagan's casual, conversational tone. An excellent article in the *Washington Post*, reported by Alec MacGillis, from the 2008 campaign trail said as much.

Obama's keynote address at the 2004 Democratic National Con-vention in Boston marked his arrival as a speaking sensation. But it exhibited only one side of him as a rhetorical performer: reading a scripted speech off a teleprompter . . . the vast majority of Obama's talking in the campaign has come in the form of the 45-minute stump speech that he has delivered, without notes, several times a day for nearly a year. . . . The stump speech is far more freewheeling than his scripted addresses. . . . Contrary to Obama's reputation as a fiery orator who traffics mainly in abstractions, much of the speech is delivered in a conversational tone.[8]

In Barack Obama's bestselling autobiography, *The Audacity of Hope*, he referenced Ronald Reagan frequently. Although the young Democrat disagrees with the Republican icon's politics repeatedly, Obama did express admiration for Reagan's gifts. "I understand his appeal," Obama wrote, referring to the Great Communicator's ability to spark Americans to "rediscover the traditional virtues of hard work, patriotism, personal responsibility, optimism, and faith. That Reagan's message found such a receptive audience spoke . . . to his skills as a communicator."[9] Obama evidently saw and adopted the fortieth president's warm, relaxed communication style in his own journey to become the forty-fourth.

The Reagan influence was clear even to the eminent conservative columnist, George Will, who in 2006 crossed party lines and recommended that Obama run for the presidency. In his national column published in the *Wall Street Journal*, Will noted that Obama shared certain key qualities with Reagan. The Republican writer praised the Democratic politician: "For a nation with jangled nerves, and repelled by political snarling, he offers a tone of sweet reasonableness. . . . Ronald Reagan, after all, demonstrated the importance of congeniality to the selling of conservatism."[10]

Barack Obama took George Will's advice—and that of many others—and carried his combination of fiery oration and sweet reasonableness onto the campaign trail. In the next chapter, you'll find a detailed analysis of the technique, style, strategy he used to create what came to be known as the "Obama phenomenon"—that *you* can use to become a Power Presenter.

CHAPTER
10

What Every Speaker Can Learn from Barack Obama

I just never heard anybody speak like him before . . . It's like he's talking to you, and not to a crowd.

—Ryan Marucco
president, Young Democrats of Macon County, Illinois[1]

Debut

Barack Obama's now-famous keynote speech at the 2004 Democratic National Convention is widely considered to be the starting point of his ascent in politics; but it was another speech two years earlier that had set his career in motion. On October 2, 2002, at the very same time that President George W. Bush and Congress were announcing their joint resolution to authorize the invasion of Iraq, Obama, then an Illinois State senator, spoke at an antiwar rally in Federal Plaza in Chicago. The *New Republic* reported an eyewitness account:

Jesse Jackson was to be the day's marquee speaker. But it was Obama, wearing a war-is-not-an-option lapel pin, who stole the show. Obama's 926-word speech denounced a "dumb war. A rash war. A war based not on reason but on passion, not on principle but on politics." The crowd was electrified. "I stood there and listened to him give that speech and said, 'Who is this guy?'" says Jennifer Spitz, one of the rally's organizers. Eventually, Spitz says, she turned to the person next to her and declared: "He needs to be president!"[2]

A year and a half later, in March 2004, Obama electrified the Democratic Party. In a fiercely contested primary election among seven candidates for the U.S. Senate seat from Illinois (a key state in the upcoming presidential election), Obama emerged the winner, with 53 percent of the vote, while his closest competitor had only 23 percent.[3] Not long after that Senator John Kerry, the party's 2004 presidential nominee, invited the rising star to deliver the keynote speech at the national convention and gave him his shot at glory.

In May 2004, two months before that watershed convention speech, the *New Yorker* magazine ran a lengthy profile on Barack Obama and his run for the U.S. Senate. The article, presciently titled "The Candidate,"[4] described Obama's charismatic effect on voters in Illinois. Large sections of the story could have run virtually intact during the 2008 presidential primaries and election by merely substituting voters across the country for those in Illinois, each group responding positively to Obama's superior speaking skills.

The Obama Phenomenon

The 2008 presidential campaign, one of the longest and most fiercely fought in the history of politics, focused extensively on Senator Barack Obama's strengths as a public speaker and his rock-star appeal. His main opponent for the Democratic nomination, Senator Hillary Rodham Clinton, frequently attacked his magnetic allure. Her Web

site charged that "his campaign is about 'just words.'"[5] She positioned
their differences as "talk versus action." Even his Republican opponent, Senator John McCain, warned voters not be "deceived by an
eloquent but empty call for change."[6]

But it was Obama's ability to deliver his call for change with such
power that it propelled him from obscurity to superstar, from underdog
to nominee, and, ultimately, from nominee to winner. His dynamic
trajectory in the primaries against Clinton is tracked by the converging
lines in the graph shown in Figure 10.1 from www.realclearpolitics.com
(RCP), an aggregation Web site that compiled an average of several
public opinion polls, including Gallup, *USA Today*, CBS/*New York
Times*, CNN, and Fox News.[7]

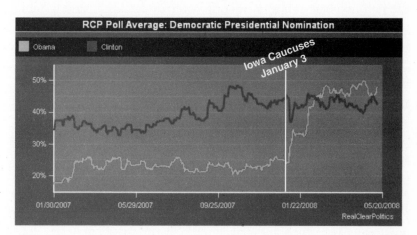

Figure 10.1　RCP Poll Average: Democratic Presidential Nomination

The graph begins in January 2007, a full year before the nation's
first primary contest and a week before Barack Obama formally
announced his candidacy. At that point, Hillary Clinton, one of
many strong Democratic contenders, was widely considered the party's
presumptive nominee. She had the organization, the relationships, the
base, the war chest, and a 34.6 percent public opinion poll advantage
over all the other candidates, more than double Obama's 17.6 percent.

One year later, on January 3, 2008, in the first official test of the presidential campaign, the Iowa caucuses, Obama made a surprise first-place finish, with 37.6 percent of the vote, while Clinton placed third, with 29.5 percent. On February 14, just six weeks after his Iowa win, Obama's sharply rising poll averages crossed Clinton's falling ratings, giving him the lead the first time, with a 45.1 percent rating to her 43.9 percent. His dramatic ascent continued with a string of 11 consecutive victories that drove all the other Democratic candidates out of the race except Clinton.

At that point, the primary campaign became an intense political contest peppered with a relentless barrage of negative charges and countercharges flying across the media and the Web. The two candidates battled fiercely across the country, state by state, and as they did, the poll numbers swung constantly, alternately closing and widening the narrow gap between them. Ultimately, Obama prevailed and became the Democratic presidential nominee. He went on to engage in an equally, if not more intense contest with John McCain, the Republican nominee. That campaign was also characterized by widely swinging poll numbers.

The plethora of factors that propelled these swings included: surprise revelations, unintentional gaffes, questionable statements, controversial relationships, inflammatory ads, media hyperbole, an economic crisis, platform maneuvering, influential endorsements, polarized voter blocs, and the Byzantine complexities of the political process—all of which are outside the scope of this book.

What is important for our purposes is that Obama, an unknown state legislator with limited experience, made two successful runs: first against Clinton, a presumptive front-runner with deep pockets and substantial credentials, and then against McCain, a lionized war hero with equally substantial credentials. Obama's remarkable bullet train ascension began with his memorable 16-minute 25-second speech and continued on to the Democratic nomination, and presidency, largely because of the electorate's positive response to his outstanding speaking skills, the positive *audience perception* of his powerful *presenter behavior.*

The Power Presenter

In chapter 5, you read that the adage "Good speakers are born not made" is a self-defeating *mis*conception that can impede your learning process. Change is indeed possible, as you saw in the examples of Presidents George W. Bush and Bill Clinton, each of whom made significant changes and improvements in his delivery style.

Barack Obama is, by any standard, a very good, if not a great, speaker. But his talent did not spring from birth or from mystical magical powers. "There was a perception that this is a very gifted individual who has a way with words," one of his former classmates told the *Washington Post.* But, the classmate went on to say, "These rhetorical and oratorical gifts have clearly developed and reached their full flower in the course of his adult political career."[8]

Obama uses a set of quite accessible techniques that you, too, can use, and which you have already learned in this book. Let's complete our analysis of the Obama phenomenon by revisiting the highlights of several key chapters, to identify the behavior that he employed to produce such positive responses—behavior that you can readily adopt.

Chapter 4: Verbalization

This chapter dealt with the powerful but underutilized technique of Verbalization: refining a presentation by speaking it aloud in rehearsal. Barack Obama practices Verbalization. The *Washington Post* story about Obama's speaking style quoted his own words.

"My general attitude is practice, practice, practice," he said in an interview. "I was just getting more experienced and seeing what is

(continued)

working and what isn't, when I am going too long and when it is going flat. Besides campaigning, I have always said that one of the best places for me to learn public speaking was actually teaching— standing in a room full of 30 or 40 kids and keeping them engaged, interested, and challenged."[9]

Chapter 6: Person-to-Person, Head Nods, Read the Reaction/Adjust Your Content

This chapter focused on connecting with individual members of your audience by engaging in person-to-person conversations and evoking head nods. Barack Obama had these techniques down pat in his run for the Illinois senate seat in 2004. The prescient *New Yorker* profile gave two relevant examples. The first came at an event for a receptive Young Democrats club in a community center in Macon County, Illinois. After Obama's speech, Ryan Marucco, the president of the group said, "I just never heard anybody speak like him before. . . . It's like he's talking to you, and not to a crowd."

And then, when speaking to a less receptive audience, a group of AFL–CIO building tradesmen who had supported his opponent in the state primary, Obama adjusted his content to include a prolabor message. The result: "Heads began nodding slowly, jaws set, as he drove his points home."[10]

Chapter 6: Think "You"

In the chapter 6 discussion of the persuasive word "you," you read how Barack Obama used that word strategically throughout his campaign for the Democratic nomination: on his Web site, in his speeches, and particularly in his speech following his surprising victory in Iowa. While the primary focus of this book is how to present your message, the message itself is an inextricable part of the package. Think of the two components as "what you say and how you say it."

To demonstrate Obama's talent as a public speaker, I have concentrated on his delivery skills; but to be thorough, it is also important to address his narrative skills. Unlike most other politicians, Obama is known to take a firm hand in crafting his texts rather than delegating the task to speech writers. In doing so, he demonstrates one of the story development techniques you learned in chapter 4: ownership. Notably, Obama wrote the landmark 2004 keynote himself.

Throughout his speeches, he uses many of the same classic rhetorical techniques used by other masters of the oratory game. For our purposes, we will focus primarily on his 2004 speech, and only on five of the tropes he has employed effectively:

- Antithesis
- Alliteration
- Anaphora
- Anecdote
- Topspin

Note

I am grateful to the excellent American Rhetoric Web site (www.americanrhetoric.com) for the formal definitions of the first four techniques.

Antithesis

Antithesis is a figure of balance in which two contrasting ideas are intentionally juxtaposed, usually through parallel structure; a contrasting of opposing ideas in adjacent phrases, clauses, or sentences.

Abraham Lincoln's Gettysburg Address contained antithetical juxtapositions:

The world will little note, nor long remember what we say here, but it can never forget what they did here.[11]

And so did John F. Kennedy's inaugural address:

And so, my fellow Americans: ask not what your country can do for you, ask what you can do for your country. My fellow citizens of the world: ask not what America will do for you, but what together we can do for the freedom of man.[12]

And so did Barack Obama's 2004 keynote:

There is not a liberal America and a conservative America—there is the United States of America.[13]

Alliteration

Alliteration is a form of emphasis that occurs through the repetition of initial consonant letters (or sounds) in two or more different words across successive sentences, clauses, or phrases.

Note the recurrence of "s" sounds in John F. Kennedy's inaugural address:

So let us begin anew—remembering on both sides that civility is not a sign of weakness, and sincerity is always subject to proof.[14]

Note the recurrence of "p" sounds in Obama's 2004 keynote:

Do we participate in a politics of cynicism or do we participate in a politics of hope?[15]

Also note the recurrence of "p" sounds in his victory speech on Election Day, November 4, 2008:

Let's resist the temptation to fall back on the same partisanship, pettiness, and immaturity that has poisoned our politics for so long.[16]

Anaphora

Anaphora (also known as a *mantra*) is a form of repetition that occurs when the first word or set of words in one sentence, clause, or phrase is/are repeated at or very near the beginning of successive sentences, clauses, or phrases; repetition of the initial word(s) over successive phrases or clauses.

In a World War II speech, Sir Winston Churchill, the British prime minister repeated the words "we shall" 11 times in successive phrases in one paragraph:

We shall not flag or fail. We shall go on to the end. We shall fight in France, we shall fight on the seas and oceans, we shall fight with growing confidence and growing strength in the air, we shall defend our island, whatever the cost may be, we shall fight on the beaches, we shall fight on the landing grounds, we shall fight in the fields and in the streets, we shall fight in the hills; we shall never surrender.[17]

In his historic civil rights speech, Reverend Martin Luther King, Jr., used the phrase "I have a dream" 16 times successively.

In his 2004 speech Obama used the word "if" in five consecutive phrases (see chapter 2, page 23 for text).

Four years later, as the presumptive Democratic nominee Obama made a whirlwind tour of the Middle East and Europe. Rhetorician that he is, Obama was quite familiar with President John F. Kennedy's historic visit to Berlin, and his celebrated "Ich bin ein Berliner" speech.

On June 26, 1963, Kennedy, standing in the shadow of the infamous Berlin Wall, addressed an enormous crowd and lauded the city as a bastion of freedom against rising the tide of Communism. During his speech, Kennedy used anaphora to extend an invitation to the world by saying "Let them come to Berlin" four times.

Forty-five years and one month later, on July 24, 2008, Obama addressed a multitude of people, estimated to number more than 200,000. He evoked Kennedy by also lauding the city and extending his own invitation to the world by echoing the phrase "Look at Berlin" in six successive sentences in his speech.

Anecdote

Anecdote is a brief human interest story, *not* a joke.

Ronald Reagan made the anecdote a hallmark of most of his speeches, frequently referencing specific citizens and their heartwarming stories to illustrate his own larger points. In fact, Reagan established the practice, since emulated by other presidents, of inviting outstanding citizens to sit in the gallery of the House Chamber during his State of the Union addresses and rise to be recognized during the speech.

Similarly, in his 2004 keynote, Barack Obama used an anecdote that referenced a human interest story, but only verbally.

I met a young man named Shamus in a VFW hall who was heading to Iraq the following week. And as I listened to him explain why he'd enlisted, the absolute faith he had in our country and its leaders, his devotion to duty and service, I thought this young man was all that any of us might ever hope for in a child.[18]

Topspin

In chapter 6 you read about Topspin, a statement that adds value in the form of a benefit or a call to action. One of Obama's key rhetorical strengths is consistency of message. His entire campaign was focused on a call for change. During the final presidential debate on October 15, 2008, in his closing statement Obama recapped the changes he was proposing and then concluded with Topspin.

I'm absolutely convinced we can do it. I would ask for your vote, and I promise you that if you give me the extraordinary honor of serving as your president, I will work every single day, tirelessly, on your behalf and on the behalf of the future of our children.[19]

Twenty days later, the voters gave him the extraordinary honor of serving as their president.

Chapter 7: Speak with Your Body Language

In this chapter, you learned a single composite skill, ERA, Eye *Connect*, Reach out, and Animation, that brings together all the key elements of delivery in one unified action. Here, each of the component parts merits a brief reference as it applies to Barack Obama's style.

Eye Connect. Barack Obama's strong Eye *Connect* is apparent in every type of speaking situation, but particularly when he speaks from a teleprompter. In such settings, the text of a speech is scrolled on two transparent Plexiglas panels simultaneously, each positioned flanking the lectern, allowing the speaker to see the text and still make Eye *Connect* with the audience. By moving back and forth between the two panels, the speaker can address all sections of the audience. But these swings can create a ping-pong effect.

Senator John McCain, Barack Obama's opponent in the presidential campaign, notoriously struggled with his teleprompter speeches because he moved abruptly, sounded choppy and darted his eyes. Whenever Barack Obama spoke from a teleprompter, he moved between the panels at logical points in the text, creating a fluid cadence, making his moves smooth and his Eye *Connect* steady.

Reach out. Barack Obama rarely extends his arms fully, except in large venues, as in his 2004 keynote. In fact, when he gestures to express himself, and he gestures quite often, he usually keeps his movements contained. A report in *Time* observed, "He's famed for his oratory, but watching him speak, you suspect he leaves about 30 percent of the emotion on the table, wary of playing the Pentecostal preacher. Physically, he is uncommonly restrained: he keeps his hands close to his head, and his shoulders are always tight and squared."[20]

This characteristic was picked up by Fred Armisen, the actor on *Saturday Night Live* who portrays Obama in the skits on the comedy series. As any impressionist would do, Armisen exaggerated those confined gestures. Armisen also exaggerated Obama's crisp, controlled cadence by speaking in a clipped staccato.

In his 2008 Election Day victory speech, standing before an immense crowd spread out before him in Grant Park in Chicago, Obama rarely extended his arms beyond the width or height of his shoulders.

Animation. In all settings, large and small, Obama is always animated, his face expressive, breaking into a ready smile or striking a serious mien, as appropriate. His voice animates musically, expressing the meaning of his words with passionate emphasis. The *Washington Post* profile describes how he gets his message across: "What audience members tend to remember are the handful of crescendos that punctuate it, which deliver all the more punch for how slowly he builds them."[21]

Chapter 8: Control Your Cadence, Complete the Arc

In the heat of the 2008 primary campaign, a controversial issue arose concerning the pastor of Obama's church in Chicago. On March 18,

Obama addressed the issue in a televised speech. Because of the subject, the event drew a great deal of attention. By the end of that week, the video of the speech had drawn almost 2.5 million hits on YouTube.[22]

It also drew a tidal wave of commentary from legions of rabid supporters as well as detractors who argued vehemently about the points of view in the content. Nonetheless, they all agreed that Obama's delivery of the speech was exceptional. As I watched and listened to the television broadcast, I did what I suggested you do when you watch the video of Ronald Reagan's final State of the Union address on our Web site: I closed my eyes and listened to Obama's cadence, isolating his Vocal dynamics from the Visual. I did the same when I listened to his Election Day victory speech live, and then later in a replay on YouTube.

Emulating Reagan, Obama rolls out his words in long arcs, like a ship riding the waves on the high seas, Completing each Arc by dropping his voice, and punctuating each point forcefully. The pauses between the arcs allows his listeners to absorb the meaning of his words, if not to become captivated by his compelling rhythm.

Another benefit of his long arcs was pointed out by Peggy Noonan, a former speechwriter for Presidents Reagan and George H. W. Bush, and now a political columnist for the *Wall Street Journal* as well as the author of a book called *On Speaking Well*.

This left TV producers having to use longer-than-usual sound bites in order to capture his meaning. And so the cuts of the speech you heard on the news were more substantial and interesting than usual, which made the coverage of the speech better.[23]

But Barack Obama did not Complete the Arc as well in less structured situations.

On August 16, 2008, Obama, by then the Democratic nominee, met John McCain for their first encounter of the presidential election at the Civil Forum on Leadership and Compassion at Saddleback Church in Orange County, California.

The event, organized and moderated by Rick Warren, the pastor of the evangelical mega church, was not a debate; Warren gave each candidate his own hour to respond to an identical set of questions. In fact, the two candidates were on stage at the same time for only a moment when Obama, who had just concluded his portion, was about to depart and McCain was about to start his. However, the format provided a virtual confrontation of their differing positions.

During Obama's hour, McCain, as Warren explained, waited in a "cone of silence," so that he would have no advance knowledge of the questions. There was no need for such measures because McCain, as did Obama, responded to all the questions with their previously established and often-stated positions on the issues. There were no surprises in their content.

There was a surprise, however, in their individual delivery styles. For months, the media had painted Barack Obama as the silver-tongued orator and John McCain as the stiff, error-prone, volatile curmudgeon. At Saddleback, their roles reversed.

Obama's answers rambled into deep erudite analyses and long nuanced discussions. His rambles were exacerbated by a proliferation of "ums," "ahs," and "y'knows," that made his answers seem even longer. McCain, on the other hand, true to his "Straight Talk Express" slogan, made his responses prompt and succinct.

The realclearpolitics.com public opinion polls you saw earlier in this chapter that tracked Obama versus Hillary Clinton (Fig 10.1) continued beyond the primaries to track Obama versus McCain. On the morning of the Saddleback debate, the RCP aggregation of 8 different polls had Obama ahead by 3.2 points. One week after the event, his lead had dropped to a virtual dead heat of 1.4 points.

But less than two weeks later, Obama returned to a milieu like that of his initial success. In 2004, the Democratic National Convention had been held indoors at the Fleet Center in Boston; in 2008, for Obama's acceptance speech, they moved outdoors to the larger Invesco Stadium in Denver. Standing before 85,000 spectators and 30 million television viewers, Obama returned to his oratorical form. Gone were the nuances, and gone were the "ums."

The next morning, Obama's lead in the RCP average bounced back up to 3.5. A still better measure was a review of the speech by Ed Rollins who provided his own credentials along with his compliments.

I've been in politics for 40 years. I had the privilege of serving Ronald Reagan as his White House political director and campaign manager, and during those years, I heard him give hundreds of speeches. And no one was ever better—The Democrats now have their own version of an RR orator.[24]

Presenter Behavior/Audience Perception

After that successful acceptance speech, the election campaign moved into high gear. Obama and McCain crisscrossed the country delivering their respective messages in every kind of presentation setting, the most critical of which were three formal presidential debates. Those direct encounters involve a unique set of point/counterpoint argumentation skills that are outside the purview of this book.* However, Barack Obama's core speaking skills demonstrate his expert command of the Visual, Vocal, and Verbal dynamics,

---

* You can find Q&A skills covered in greater detail in my book, *In the Line of Fire: How to Handle Tough Questions*.

and he does it all with the very same techniques available to you or to any speaker.

Barack Obama does not use slides in his presentations, nor did Ronald Reagan or any of the other masters of the game. National leaders and politicians, due to the highly sensitive nature of their words, usually speak from prepared texts or from carefully vetted and rehearsed position statements, but without slides. In contrast, in virtually every other walk of life, Microsoft PowerPoint has become the medium of choice for presentations and speeches, and so it is important to consider how you integrate your slides with your delivery skills. Yet, until this point in the book, you have not read a single word of advice about that integration—intentionally.

I have treated the development of your Eye *Connect*, body language, and voice skills in modules, just as you do when you learn to swim. You start out on dry land, at the side of the pool, and learn the arm strokes separate from the leg strokes. Then you get into the pool at the shallow end, where you practice the arm strokes separate from the leg strokes. Not until you become proficient in the all basics do you put them together and start to swim in deeper water.

Now, it's time for you to get into the presentation water, to combine your delivery skills and your slides in a vital skill called Graphics Synchronization, the subject of the next chapter.

11

Graphics Synchronization

G raphics Synchronization is a close cousin of graphics design. Design is what you *show*, or what your audience sees displayed by your PowerPoint slideshow; synchronization is what you *do* (your eyes and body language) and *say* (your voice) when you show what you show; Graphics Synchronization is the integration of your slides with your Visual and Vocal components. All these factors exist in a teeterboard relationship, as in Figure 11.1.

Figure 11.1 Graphics Synchronization

If what you show is designed in adherence to the Less Is More principle, the slide will speak for itself instantly. Your audience will understand it as soon as it appears. They won't have to think about the image. You will have very little to do and say to explain it to your audience. The teeterboard will tilt in your favor, as in Figure 11.2.

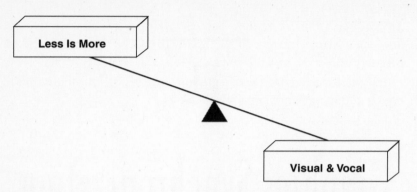

Figure 11.2   Less Is More Design Makes Less for You to do and Say

In fact, you will be free to go beyond the content shown on your slide and add value by interpreting it, or citing examples, case studies, statistics, anecdotes, endorsements, or offering benefits.

On the other hand, if your graphics are designed under the More Is Less principle, as top-heavy, cluttered eye charts, your audience will not understand your slide. You will have to *do* and *say* a great deal to explain it to them, as in Figure 11.3.

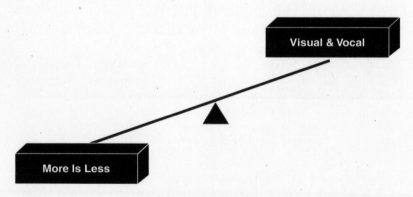

Figure 11.3   More Is Less Design Makes More for You to Do and Say

The teeterboard will tilt against you. Your audience will dart their eyes back and forth between you and the screen, trying to understand your complex slide and what it has to do with what you are saying.

You will see their confusion, become anxious, and your adrenaline flow will accelerate. You will go into overdrive, blathering away like a neurotic character in a Woody Allen movie, trying to explain your slide. Under these stressful circumstances, it is doubtful that you will ever get around to adding any value.

Less Is More slides would solve only half the problem. The other half of the solution comes from a familiar skill set, the classic:

- Tell 'em What You're Gonna Tell 'em.
- Tell 'em.
- Tell 'em What You've Told 'em.

As important as these instructions are in *telling* your story, they are even more important in *showing* your story. That is because the human eye is more sensitive than the human ear. If your audience gets lost as you tell your story, they can easily think about it, regroup, and then catch up with you. But if their eyes become absorbed in trying to interpret a bright new image, crammed with excessive data, projected onto a large screen, their eyes, and minds, will become so overloaded, they will disconnect from you and from the mission-critical message you are trying to convey. And they will never catch up.

The solution: Adapt the classic skill set:

Tell 'em, *Show* 'em, Tell 'em

- Tell 'em What You're Gonna *Show* 'em.
- *Show* 'em.
- Tell 'em What You've *Shown* 'em.

Let's examine at each of these three instructions in greater detail.

Tell 'em What You're Gonna Show 'em means create a *transition* between slides. We've all seen the presenters who jabber away at one rate while their slides flit by on the screen at a completely different rate. There is no relationship between what they are saying and what they are showing. It's like watching a film with a soundtrack out of synchronization with the image. You see a character's lips moving, but the words lag behind. This is disruptive in a film and equally so in a presentation.

Federico Fellini was one of the world's greatest film directors, but he focused more on images than on voice. As a result, he cast actors, often nonprofessionals, for their appearance rather than their voices, and later dubbed their dialogue with the voices of professional actors. But Fellini's dubbing wasn't always as thorough as his camerawork, and watching his films where the actors' lips move slightly out of synchronization is distracting; made even more distracting by the additional images of the English subtitles of the Italian dialogue popping on and off at the bottom of the screen. Fortunately, Fellini's films provide a vast treasure of other redeeming qualities rarely offered by any presenter.

One way to create a transition between slides is to make a *closure* statement about the outbound image. Say something conclusive about the slide currently on the screen. "From this timeline, you can see that our company's operational efficiencies and productivity gains have reduced our costs." The end. Closure.

Another transitional option is to lead to the upcoming slide. "Now let's take a look at how that cost reduction is reflected our head-count." That is a *direct lead* and it presupposes that you are absolutely certain that the headcount slide is next. Do not try this trick at home unless you are absolutely certain. Otherwise, you will experience that dreadful moment when your mind goes totally blank. You suddenly get that sinking feeling in your stomach, and you say to yourself, "Yikes! What's next? Is it the head-count slide or the growth strategy slide?" You certainly don't want to do a direct lead to the head-count slide only to have the growth strategy slide pop onto the screen. This embarrassing instant is usually accompanied by a nervous "Ahem . . . .!" followed a rushed, mumbled apology, "But first, let's look at our growth strategy!"

This awkward moment can happen whether you are presenting your slide show for the first time or the one hundred and first time. It can happen with a presentation that has been thrust into your hands only moments before the start or with a presentation you have delivered so many times you are on autopilot. When that "Yikes!" moment strikes, you will feel an egg dribble slowly and uncontrollably down your chin.

A third transitional option is the *indirect lead.* "Let's take another look at our company story." Now you have three transitions choices:

- Closure on the outbound slide.
- Direct lead to the inbound slide.
- Indirect lead to the inbound slide.

The easiest, safest, and simplest of the three is closure. Any one of them concludes your discussion of the outbound slide and leaves your audience primed for the inbound slide. Fulfill that priming by clicking to display your next graphic: **Show 'em**.

At the precise moment of the click, you yield complete control of your presentation to a greater power: the eyes of your audience. The instant a large, bright new image pops onto the screen, every pair of eyes in the room will ratchet over to look at it involuntarily. Their response to the new image is a *reflex* action.

To demonstrate the power of this reflex, try this simple exercise. Turn to a person sitting next to you and look him or her straight in the eye. Then extend your left arm out away from your body, start flapping your hand, and say to that person, "Don't look at my left hand!" He or she will be unable to comply.

I conduct a similar exercise with the participants in my coaching sessions. On my laptop computer screen, I build a list of bulleted words and then click backward in PowerPoint to remove the last word in the build. Then I tell everyone that I am going to click forward to make that word reappear and ask them *not* to look at the screen. After all, they have just seen the word, they know what is coming, and so there is no need to look. Inevitably, as soon as I click, they look. The power of their optic reflexes makes it impossible to keep from looking at one word reappearing on a 15-inch computer screen.

When a large group of people in an audience sees 50 or so brand-new words pop onto a 150-inch projection screen *for the first time*, reflexively their eyes will ratchet over to take in all the words. At that same point in time, most presenters, driven by their accelerated adrenaline flow, keep talking.

What does the audience hear of what the presenter is saying? *Nothing.*

Actually, worse than nothing, more likely, complete gibberish. Because the audience's eyes are focused on the screen, reading silently at a rate faster than even the FedEx man can speak; any words the presenter says become asynchronous with the slide. The eyes and ears of the audience become conflicted. The effect is similar to what happens when the video and audio cables of a camcorder are crisscrossed: disturbing static.

What should the presenter do instead? *Pause.*

How will the pause feel to the presenter? *Uncomfortable.* Time warp again.

How will that discomfort look to the audience? *They will not even notice.* Their eyes will be busy taking in the large, bright, demanding image on the projection screen.

Olivier Fontana, a group product manager in Microsoft's Embedded Business Unit, travels a great deal, making presentations on behalf of the company. On one of his more demanding international trips, Olivier often had to present while fighting jet lag. At one point during one of his presentations, he clicked to a new slide and turned to look at it on his computer screen. Just then, he felt himself beginning to nod off. He caught himself, but panicked, thinking that his audience had seen him. But when he turned to look at them, he saw that they were so engrossed in the slide on his computer screen they were not looking at him.

This is not to suggest that nodding off during your presentation is acceptable, but to be aware that your audience will look at your graphic reflexively, and so you can allow yourself to pause without panicking.

What might you be doing during the eternity of that seemingly interminable pause, other than twisting slowly, slowly in the wind, or fighting or fleeing? *Thinking would help.*

What would enable your thinking? *Look at your slide.*

Look at your slide while your audience is looking at it. In that instant, you will recognize the slide and know just what to say about it. In computer technology, this is known as *screen refresh*. In presentations, your mind is the screen, and it becomes refreshed with the next topic of your presentation.

Title *Plus*

When you look at the new slide, look at it in its entirety. This overview is called Title *Plus*. The title serves as the headline for the whole slide. In addition to the title, however, there are additional elements: a bar chart or a pie chart, a timeline, a photograph, a map, an icon, a logo, or a set of bullets. That is the *Plus*. Look at the Title *Plus* of each slide. For example, if the title is "Revenue Growth," see it *plus* the five revenue bars; if the title is "Growth Strategy," see it *plus* the four lines of bullets.

To review, all of the following happens while you **Show 'em**:

- *Click* to your inbound slide.
- Your audience looks at it in a *reflex* action.

- *Pause* as they do.
- *Look at your slide* during your pause.
- See the whole slide as Title *Plus*.

Once you've looked at your new slide, you will immediately recognize it and know just what to say about it. (You will, even if the presentation was thrust into your hands just minutes or hours before the Moment of Truth, and you had only enough time to click through the slides once, rapidly.) Your audience, however, will not have a clue about the slide. Your job is to **Tell 'em What You've Shown 'em.**

As that inbound slide appears, describe it to them. Tell 'em what you saw. State the Title *Plus*: "This slide represents the strong growth of our product revenues over five years." Or, "These are the actions we plan to take to continue that revenue growth."

Once you've told your audience what you've shown 'em, and they've seen what you've shown 'em, they will turn away from the screen and look back at you. Your words will have filled in the blank slates of their minds. Now that they are clear about the slide, all their attention will focus on you, ready to listen to whatever you have to say.

With the Title *Plus*, you will have to say less about the slide itself; in fact, you can go on to *add value* beyond the information shown on the slide. You can interpret, analyze, offer supporting evidence, cite case studies, make a call to action, give your audience WIIFYs—you can deliver an oration. One Title *Plus* gives you multiple WIIFYs.

Note

Telling 'em What You've Shown 'em provides an additional benefit. It obviates the practice of hitting the "B" or "W" key on the computer to black out or white out the screen during the presentation. Some presenters use this little-known PowerPoint feature to draw attention away from the screen and to themselves; the feature is a vestige of the old days of overhead and 35mm projectors, when presenters hit the off switch in the middle of their slide show, causing a sudden loud sound and a disruptive change in the lighting. If you give your audience sufficient time to look at your slide and then describe it to them, there is no need to hide your slide. With their curiosity satisfied, your audience will focus on you.

The Back Link

Let's return to that dreaded sinking-feeling-in-the-stomach moment. You have just finished your discussion of the outbound cost reduction timeline slide and you suddenly say to yourself, "Yikes! What's next? Is it the head-count slide or the growth strategy?" Suddenly, you realize that a direct lead is very risky.

Don't panic: Simply make a brief closure statement about the outbound slide. "From this timeline, you can see that our company's operational efficiencies and productivity gains have reduced our costs." Pause. Then click, turn, and look at the screen. The head-count slide pops on. *Whew!* Now you know.

You can then Back Link to the prior slide by saying, "Here's how that cost reduction is reflected in our head-count," restating a word from the title of the prior slide.

The Back Link is drawn from a literary technique where, by repeating a word or a phrase from the preceding paragraph (the outbound) in the subsequent paragraph (the inbound), the writer creates continuity between the two paragraphs.

A personal example: This book is based on concepts that I have evolved over two decades in the Power Presentations program. In adapting the material for the book, my editor suggested that I shift a particular section from one chapter to another, a position in the book different from where it exists in the program. I struggled with the move until I found a phrase in the last paragraph in the new chapter and repeated it at the beginning of the newly shifted paragraph; the change worked.

Create continuity between your inbound and outbound slides with a Back Link.

Contrast the Back Link with the maddeningly rote transition that most presenters use as they churn through their slides. They finish the timeline slide then click and say, "Now I'd like to talk about the headcount." When they finish the headcount slide, they click and say, "Now I'd like to talk about the growth strategy."

This "Now I'd like to . . ." approach causes a backfire rather than a Back Link because it provides absolutely no continuity. It restarts the presentation with every slide, forcing your audience to work hard to keep up with you. *If you make it hard for your audience, they will make it hard for you.*

Therefore, the Back Link has a double benefit:

- Your audience can more easily follow your narrative flow.
- You do not have to remember what comes next. Trying to memorize the sequence of your slides is a complete waste of time, energy, and memory capacity.

Finally, to whom should you be delivering that Back Link? *One person.*

To summarize, all of the following happens while you **Tell 'em What You've Shown 'em:**

- Describe.
- Title *Plus*.

- Add Value.
- Back Link.
- One Person.

To review the whole process, please see the table in Figure 11.4.

Tell 'em	Show 'em	Tell 'em
Transition	Click	Describe
Closure	Reflex	Title *Plus*
Lead	Pause	...add value
Direct	Look @ Slide	Back Link
Indirect	Title *Plus*	One Person

Figure 11.4 Graphics Synchronization

There are 15 instructions in this table, but you will never be able to remember all of them. Nor can you take this book up to the front of the room with you, so let's distill them into a simple takeaway.

Speak Only to Eyes

This is precisely the same instruction you learned in chapter 8 as the distillation of the Phrase and Pause skill. Graphics Synchronization is essentially an extension of Phrase and Pause. It provides the cadence and the logic to move from person to person during your presentation. Speak Only to Eyes. The same concept holds true with your slides. There are no eyes on your projection screen.

This is a positive way of saying, "Do not speak to the screen," but that is aversion therapy again. Speak Only to Eyes. When you Speak Only to Eyes, and *not* the screen, you avoid three damaging pitfalls.

- Turning your back to the audience.
- Muffling the acoustics of your voice.
- Reading the slide verbatim.

The last pitfall is the most damaging. It inevitably irritates your audience because they think, "I can read it myself! Don't waste my time!" Reading the slide verbatim sends the message that the presenter is speaking down to, or patronizing, the audience. Even worse, reading the slide triggers a deeply ingrained universal habit: The first time anyone ever read to you was to put you to sleep; thus you—and every person in every audience you will ever face—are forever programmed.

Reading the slide also sends the message that you need a crutch, which implies that you have not prepared very well or that you do not know your material; either implication diminishes your credibility.

Reading the slide has one final negative impact: It sets up the anticipation that you are going to read the entire slide. Even if it is a Less Is More slide, your audience will think, "This is going to take forever!"

Instead, paraphrase, use synonyms, or juxtapose the key words in the Title. Your audience can easily make the interpolation. Then add other words for the *Plus* (bars, pie, bullet, etc.). For instance, with the example of the timeline slide, if the title reads: "Cost Reduction Results," your Title *Plus* could be, "Here's how our company's operational efficiencies have reduced our costs over the last six quarters." If the title of the slide reads "Growth Strategy," your Title *Plus* could be, "These four steps are how we intend to continue to grow our company."

The Power of the Pause

Of the 15 instructions in Figure 11.4, the most difficult will be the pause. Time warp makes the pause seem like an eternity, but only for you, not for your audience. They need the pause to take in your slide.

In Phrasing and Pausing in chapter 8, you learned that the pause has 10 benefits. In Graphics Synchronization, the pause takes on two new valuable aspects.

- Your audience reads reflexively.
- You get a prompt.

However, the prompt function will be lost if you are not mindful of the design of your slides. If your slides are eye charts, you will have to pause longer to allow your audience to take in all the information. The eternity of time warp will then multiply to infinity and the adrenaline will start rushing through your body. If you design Less Is More slides,* your pause will be shorter and you will minimize the time warp, which will make you feel *and* appear calmer.

The First Time

After the pause, the next most difficult instruction for you will be to look at the slide. You may be at either end of the presentation preparation spectrum:

- You have created and rehearsed your slide show thoroughly and know each slide cold.
- You had the presentation thrust into your hands just minutes or hours before the Moment of Truth and had only time enough to click through the slides rapidly.

In either case, when you click to any given slide in the presentation, you will instantly recognize it and say to yourself, "Oh, *that* one!"

But the potential investor or customer or partner or key decision maker in your audience has never seen the slide before. Such people do not like to be rushed into making decisions. You must give them the

---

*You can find detailed guidelines for all presentation graphics in my book, *Presenting to Win*.

time to absorb the new image. *Look at the new slide as if you have never seen it.* See it as if it is for the *first time*. The French call this *jamais vu,* never seen.

If you rush (and your adrenaline will certainly drive you to do so) to turn back to look at your audience, you very likely see that they are still reading the slide and are not looking back at you. That will instantly trigger the sinking-feeling-in-the-stomach moment and unleash more adrenaline. The cascade gathers momentum.

Each time you turn to look at each of your slides, do it as if you are seeing it for the first time.

When you turn to look, the relative position of you and your slide comes into play.

Tools of the Presentation Trade

There are many tools of the presentation trade: screens, microphones, lecterns, projectors, computers, and remote control devices. The first three are standard operating equipment in almost every respectable conference room on the planet; the latter three are in a constant state of technological flux. All six must be carefully integrated with each presenter's or speaker's Graphics Synchronization skills. Unfortunately, all six are subject to the vagaries of public venue layouts and/or a lack of knowledge about how to use these tools to their maximum effect. The world is not optimal, and neither is the world of presentations, but the following guidelines can help you intervene to arrange the tools to optimize your presentation.

The guidelines are grouped according to the relationship of the presenter and the specific tool:

Presenter and Screen

- *Present with the screen at your left.* Western audiences are culturally accustomed to reading from left to right, so when you present with the screen at your left, your audience will start with you and then take in the new image in a familiar, comfortable move. This is particularly important with text slides because if the positions were reversed your audience would be forced to take in each line of text in two moves: backward with the words in reverse, and then forward on the second pass. With the screen at your left, they will easily take in the words on their first pass.

Furthermore, with the screen at your left, when you gesture or reach out to your audience, you will do it primarily with your right hand, replicating the handshake. You can use your left hand to gesture toward the screen. Both movements pump your lungs and create vocal animation.

- *Present in the screen plane.* Stand in the same-depth plane as the screen so that you can see it by looking over your left shoulder. This will keep you from turning your back to the audience to look at the screen. This positioning will also be easier on your audience, saving them from having to adjust their focus. When you are presenting seated, use the lid of your laptop computer as your screen and sit in the same plane.

- *Present at the edge of the screen.* Stand as close as possible to the screen so your audience won't have to swing their eyes a great distance from you to the screen.

- *Avoid the projection beam.* Keep your hand away from the light of the projection beam, otherwise your audience will be distracted by the unusual patterns superimposed on your hand or your face, or by the odd shadow figure your hand casts on the screen. You can gesture *toward* the screen and describe where you want your audience to look with your words. This skill is called *Verbal Navigation*, and is discussed in detail in the next chapter.

Presenter and Audience

- *Face front.* Because you Speak Only to Eyes (and because there are no eyes on the screen), you will not speak to the screen. Face front and look each person in your audience straight in the eye when you speak. In addition to the sincerity factor, when both your eyes are engaged with both eyes of another person, it creates the engagement-equals-expressiveness equation and animates your features.

- *Illuminate for Eye Connect.* Don't darken the lighting in the room to create contrast on the slides, or you will lose Eye *Connect* in the process. Sacrifice the slide image, not the Eye *Connect*.

- *Present at the eye level of the audience.* This creates a sense of intimacy and empathy. Ronald Reagan's great strength was to create the impression that he was at the same level as his audience. You can create that same impression with your audience. Note, however, that this arrangement only holds true when you are seated in presentations to small groups. In larger groups, of more than half a dozen, you will have to stand to able to see each person and make Eye *Connect*.

- If you were to stand to present or speak to a small group, you would be looking down at your audience. In cinematography and photography this is known as a *superior angle*, which is used to convey a sense of dominance; e.g., the evil giant looks down at the victim menacingly. The converse is the *inferior angle*, which is used to convey a sense of subordination; e.g., the helpless victim looks up at the giant fearfully.

- *Check sightlines.* Be sure each person in your audience can see you and the screen. You can take a slight step to make Eye *Connect* with people who are seated behind other people. Keep in mind that the screen is fixed, so be sure you have the image projected high enough so that the people in the back can see the entire image.

This comprehensive list of guidelines will take a great deal of effort to implement. With your intense focus on your time, your content, your slideshow and your adrenaline, you might be tempted to bypass attending to them. Don't. Unheeded, these factors can aggregate to make it difficult for your audience to focus on and absorb your presentation. Audience Advocacy again. Make it easy for your audience and they will make it easy for you. The converse is unacceptable.

The Lectern

Some presenters use a lectern for the following reasons:

- Hold the notes.
- Hold the microphone.
- Hold the computer.
- Hold the presenter.
- Hide the presenter.
- Promote the hotel.

Try these reasons instead:

- Use the graphics on the screen as your notes.
- Arrange for a wireless microphone.
- Use a wireless remote control to change the slides.
- Stand on your own two feet.
- Come out in the open.
- Promote yourself.

B-School Versus C-School

One of the most commonly held *false* beliefs about presentations is that if the presenter turns to look at the screen, the presenter appears not to know his or her own material. This belief arises out of business school, or B-school thinking. Be prepared.

Here is a cinema, or C-school, fact: If the presenter does not turn to look at a new slide, but continues to look at the audience, the audience will become conflicted. Their optic reflexes will demand that they look at the new image, while *simultaneously* their mirror neurons will demand that they keep returning the presenter's gaze. Driven by two opposing neurological impulses, the audience's eyes will rapidly shuttle back and forth between the screen and the presenter in confusion.

Instead, you must turn to look at the screen the instant a new image appears. As a matter of fact, *turn to look at the screen with every click on every slide*. Every time you turn to the screen, your movement will lead your audience to look where you are looking. Both you and your audience will arrive at the identical point in your presentation, in synchronization.

Every cinematographer, film editor, and director understands the powerful subconscious physiological, psychological, and social forces that impact audiences. These professionals play to these dynamics: They shoot and edit sequences rapidly to create negative tension, or slowly to create positive feelings. You want to create only positive feelings in your audiences.

At this point, another cinematic factor comes into play: computer animation. For the soft-cover and second editions of *Presenting to Win*, I added a chapter on the animation feature in PowerPoint and related it to cinematic techniques. The chapter covered the wide array of options available in the software to create motion, but I recommended that the default animation should be left to right, the direction in which people in Western culture read text. Therefore, when you turn to look at the screen—properly positioned to your left for the same cultural reason—the movement of your body will not only lead your audience to the screen but will culminate with the new graphic image entering from the same direction in one continuous—and positive— fluid movement.

For your presentations, think as they do in C-school; save the B-school thinking for your spreadsheets.

To recapitulate:

Tell 'em What You're Gonna Show 'em. Transition with one of three choices:
- Closure on the outbound slide.
- Direct lead to the inbound slide.
- Indirect lead to the inbound.

Show 'em. Display the slide and pause as you do. Turn and look at the slide as if you've never seen it, seeing the Title *Plus*. Turn back out. Find both eyes of one person.

Tell 'em What You've Shown 'em. Describe the slide using the Title *Plus* and a Back Link. Then add value galore.

Central to all of the preceding is the pause. If you design Less Is More slides, both you and your audience will have less visual information to process each time a new image appears on your screen. Your pause will be shorter and your audience will understand your graphics more rapidly. Another way to look at Graphics Synchronization is that it is *less about what you do and more about what you **don't** do. The power of the pause.*

A case in point: the Dolby Laboratories IPO road show. I was privileged to coach the company's CEO, Bill Jasper, and his executive team to develop their pitch to potential investors. We spent the better part of five days together focusing on every aspect of their presentation including the narrative structure of their story, the design and anima-tion of their slides, and body language and voice of the presenters. Most important, I coached them on how to integrate all of these essential factors.

The centerpiece of the Dolby story was their vision of what they called "The Complete Content Chain," a series of six steps that take content (for television or film) from its creation by professionals to its playback by consumers, and Dolby's role (and opportunity to generate revenues) at each of the steps. In their slide show, they depicted this chain as a series of six green rectangles arrayed in a semicircular arc, and Dolby's role at each step depicted as a series of six orange boxes, arranged in a parallel arc. Using animation to illustrate the various stages, the rectangles and boxes moved, morphed, and changed text to express the potential, implementation, and progression of the vision.

Bill Jasper decided to spread the five days of the Power Presenta-tions program over several months to give himself sufficient time to learn and practice the skills. When he was ready, we gathered in the sumptuous, state-of-the-art Dolby screening auditorium in their San Francisco offices to present our efforts to the team of investment bankers who led the offering. Because the offering was eagerly awaited by the stock market, Dolby Labs chose to take the unusual step of having two major banks, Goldman Sachs and Morgan Stanley, (usually fierce competitors) in the lead in what is known in the financial trade as *Joint Book Runners*.

In attendance at the run-through was a virtual army of bankers, ranging from corporate finance to retail sales to analysts to interns. As diverse as they may be as individuals, most people in the world of high-stress, high-stakes financial markets all share a common characteristic: a short attention span. Over the past 20 years, I have been privileged to coach more than 500 other road shows and can safely attest that none of them has ever run through a presentation without interruption. Until Dolby.

As Jasper ran through his presentation, not one man or woman in that auditorium uttered a peep. When he was done, a murmur ran through the crowd. Finally, one voice spoke up. It was one of the senior bankers, a man who had seen his fair share of road shows. His first words were, "Your graphics worked very well, and I really liked the way you paused and gave us time to read them."

Bill Jasper turned to me and smiled.

Think about that: the missing link in presentations is not what you do; it is what you don't do.

Pause.

Before we leave this powerful skill, however, let's focus in greater detail on what you do *say*—your narrative—in the next chapter.

CHAPTER

12

Graphics and Narrative

Title *Plus* in Action

Leslie Culbertson is the vice president of finance at Intel Corporation. When she assumed that role, I had the opportunity to coach her for her first major presentation at an investment conference. Leslie was a most diligent student: She took full ownership of her presentation by shaping her content, Verbalizing her narrative, and designing her own slides. As part of the process, we exchanged her slide show via email several times to refine them.

Two months later, Leslie called me early one the morning and asked, "Could you review my presentation again?"

"Sure," I replied, "go ahead and email it to me."

"Well, I can't do that," said Leslie, "I'm in the car now, on the way to the conference."

"Who's driving?" I asked.

"A colleague," said Leslie, reassuringly.

"Okay, go for it."

199

Leslie was on her mobile phone. I was in my office on a land line. She had the slides on her laptop. I did not. All I could review was her narrative.

Leslie began, "This slide represents the continuing growth of Intel's product revenues over five years." In my mind's eye, I could see five bars. Then Leslie spent about a minute discussing the reasons for the revenue growth.

"Now," she continued, "let's look at those same revenues in quarterly installments . . ." In my mind's eye I could now see 20 bars. (Note: By saying "those same revenues," incorporating a word from the preceding slide, Leslie used a Back Link instead of the conventional abrupt, "Now I'd like to talk about the quarterly revenues.") Then she went on to discuss and analyze the quarterly revenue patterns.

Leslie was using the Title *Plus* technique to introduce each slide. Her words captured the overview of each slide, encompassing the Title *Plus* the rest of the image. Once she made that opening statement, I understood the full context of the slide and, without any visual support, I was able to follow Leslie's discussion. I even had an *Aha!* moment as Leslie added value by describing how Intel expected to continue the revenue growth with new products.

Start your discussion of every slide with a Title *Plus*. It will make the rest of your narrative flow more smoothly and enable your audience to stay with you. After the Title *Plus*, however, different types of slides have different narrative follow-throughs.

Simple slides start with a Title *Plus*. Then, because your audience will understand the image instantly, you can can move on to elaborate on the material on the slide and add value.

Complex slides also start with a Title *Plus*, but then you must help your audience understand your slide by guiding them through the image. Use *Verbal Navigation*, the skill I introduced in the previous chapter. Navigate your audience's eyes with your words.

In chapter 1, during my discussion of the relative impact of presentation dynamics, I described the pie chart in Figure 1.1, as follows: "The largest wedge is in black at 55 percent; moving clockwise, the middle one in gray, is at 38 percent, and the smallest wedge is in white, at 7 percent." I navigated your eyes using shape, color, direction. I could have used compass points: north, south, and so on; or clock orientation: twelve o'clock, six o'clock; or I could have used first column, second column; I could also have used top or bottom.

Beware of left and right. Because the presenter and the audience are facing in opposite directions, left and right are different for each. Orient your audience by saying, "Here . . ." as you gesture toward the side of the screen nearest you. Or say, "There . . ." and gesture toward the side of the screen farthest from you. Using the same gesturing approach, you can say, "Near side . . ." or "Far side . . ." Or be specific and say, "On the left side of the screen . . . ," or "On the right side of the screen . . ." Tell' em What You've Shown' em.

Verbal Navigation obviates the need for pointers, a device that has inexplicably become standard equipment in the presentation trade. Don't follow the lemmings. Trash all pointers. Rigid pointers, whether the long wooden or collapsible metal type, become twirling batons, toys, wands, lances, spears, or swords in the hands of nervous presenters. Their diminutive cousins, laser pointers, produce frenetic light shows. As you grasp either type of pointer, your hand turns into a fist. Worse, grasping a pointer inhibits opening your hand when you Reach out to create a handshake.

Very complex slides also start with a Title *Plus*, but then become the exception to the rule. Certain slides require a level of detail that is irreducible: for example, financial charts, architectural diagrams, or flowcharts. You have two choices with such slides:

- *Build* the slide in stages.
- *Display all* the information on the screen at once. Then, rather than try to Eye *Connect* with your audience, turn to face the screen and narrate with your voiceover.

One final note about Title *Plus*: Begin each of your overview statements with "Here . . ." or "This . . .", or "These . . .". Each of these words causes you to reference the image on the screen immediately and specifically. "This slide represents the continuing growth of our product revenues over five years." Then you can also incorporate the powerful Back Link technique you read about in the previous chapter. After the Title *Plus*, refer back to the previous slide by saying, "All of this growth was driven by our aggressive marketing campaign." The Back Link creates flow in your presentation.

By saying "Here . . .", "This . . .", or "These . . ." as you reference the screen, you gain the opportunity to extend your left arm out to the screen (properly positioned to your left), which will produce the bellows effect that animates your voice.

The Title *Plus* and Back Link techniques combined tie your story and your slides together in a seamless narrative that makes it easy for your audience to follow. So easy, they are even able to follow your presentation when they are not present in the same room with you. To illustrate:

Dr. Katherine Crothall was the founding CEO of Animas Corporation, a company that designs, manufactures, and markets products and services for patients with insulin-requiring diabetes. Animas is now owned by Johnson & Johnson, but when it went public in the spring of 2004, Kathy engaged me to coach her IPO road show. For the final run-through of the presentation, she invited the investment bankers who were managing the offering to attend the session. Two of the bankers drove from New York City to the Animas offices in Frazer, Pennsylvania. Another banker, Eric Tardif, then of the Piper Jaffray firm, and now with Morgan Stanley, was stuck in Minneapolis because of a snowstorm that had shut down air travel. Kathy emailed the slides to Eric, and he called in on the speaker phone just as she was about to begin her presentation to the other two bankers on-site.

Eric's voice boomed on the speaker phone, "How will I know when you change slides?"

"You'll know," replied Kathy.

She then moved through her presentation using a Title *Plus* and Back Link for each slide, creating a full narrative flow.

At the end of the presentation Kathy asked Eric if he had been able to follow.

The speaker phone amplified his answer, "Absolutely!"

Kathy's firm grasp of the Title *Plus* technique, as well as all her other presentation skills, contributed to a successful road show that generated enormous investor interest. The offering of 4,250,000 shares had orders for 44 million shares—11 times oversubscribed. Animas priced at $15, the top of the anticipated $13 to $15 range, and all this during a period when the NASDAQ was down 6 percent and four of the previous five health care IPOs were trading below their offering price. A Power IPO road show presentation if there ever were one.

Bullets

What do most presenters do when they display bullets? *Read them verbatim.*

How does that make audiences feel? *I can read it myself!*

In the previous chapter, we saw how this negative behavior produces a negative perception. The solution is to paraphrase or juxtapose the key words or use synonyms. Nowhere is this more applicable than in bullet slides.

In the example shown in Figure 12.1, you can capture the entire slide by paraphrasing the Title *Plus*, "Here we see four features of our new product." Or, "Here are the key features of our new product." You can either specify the number or be general.

Figure 12.1   Bullet Slide

Once you've described the big picture, turn back to the screen, glance at the first bullet, then turn back to one person in the audience, and Tell' em What You've Shown' em by saying, again by paraphrasing, "We've improved the processing speed over the previous version . . ." Then go on and discuss the bullet: ". . . by adding a more powerful chip that provides backup protection." Go further still and add value: "This is what differentiates our product from all other products in the market."

When you are finished with your discussion of the first bullet, turn back to the screen, glance at the second bullet, then turn back to another person and say, "We've also added new options that will allow you to . . ." and continue the same discussion pattern as with the first bullet. Paraphrase, discuss, and add value.

However, if you were then to turn back to the screen and glance at the slide in Figure 12.1 and say, "We've improved the service for our product by . . ." your audience's eyes would dart back to look at the slide because you skipped a bullet. You did not acknowledge the third bullet, Greater Functionality.

This behavior produces one of several possible negative perceptions:

- You forgot.
- You don't know what to say about Greater Functionality.
- You are evading the subject because you have something to hide.
- You are rushing because you have run out of time.

The positive behavior is: *Skip No Bullets.*

The one exception to this very important rule is to treat your bullets as a group and state that in your Title *Plus*: "Here we see four features of our new product." Then go on to say that you will focus on only the last two bullets. Having given your audience the time to see all four, they will be tolerant (if not quite grateful) for your abbreviation. But please consider this exception *only* as a fallback strategy. *You will be far more effective if you address **every** bullet on every slide, or conversely, if you put **only** the bullets you will address on every slide.*

If you do use this abridgment approach, be sure that all the bullets are clearly related. You can do this by structuring them in grammatically parallel forms; begin each bullet with same part speech: all nouns, all verbs or, as in Figure 12.1, all adjectives.

Quotations

What do most presenters do when they display quotations? *Read them verbatim.*

How does that make audiences feel? *I can read it myself!*

This is another example of negative behavior that produces a negative perception. Instead, use the Title *Plus* technique. In Figure 12.2, you

> *Fourscore and seven years ago, our fathers brought forth on the continent, a new nation, conceived in liberty and dedicated to the proposition that all men are created equal.*

Figure 12.2　Abraham Lincoln's Gettysburg Address

can capture the entire slide by saying, "Here are the words of a great orator."

Then pause and, in the silence, turn to the screen and read the words as if you've never seen them, giving your audience the time to do the same. Of course, the more words on the screen, the longer the pause will be for you—in time warp—to twist slowly, slowly in the wind. The eternity is *altogether fitting and proper* for Abraham Lincoln's immortal words, but if the words are those of a garden variety More Is Less eye chart, that eternity will exceed the length of time it would take for hell to freeze over.

When you are finished reading, turn back out to engage with one member of your audience and wait until that person looks back at you, signaling that he or she is finished reading. When you see *both* of that person's eyes, Tell 'em What You've Shown 'em by saying, "This is Abraham Lincoln's famous Gettysburg Address."

Then move to another person and say, "It is not only one of the world's most famous speeches, it is also one of the world's shortest. The entire text contains a total of 272 words!"

Since that last statement is not on the slide, all of the added value comes from you. *Positive behavior, positive perception.*

Numeric and Relational Graphics

Numbers and tables have special considerations. Start with a Title *Plus*, as always, but then help your audience to understand the slide by defining the vertical and horizontal axes. In chapter 2, I described the Effectiveness Matrix in Figure 2.2 as follows: "[T]he story effectiveness is charted on the vertical axis from low up to high, and the delivery effectiveness is charted on the horizontal axis from low out to high."

Use the Verbal Navigation technique, too. "The blue indicates . . ." or "The yellow indicates . . ." or "The first column represents . . ." or "On the top row you'll see . . ."

Once you have oriented your audience to your graphic, you can then move on to discuss the chart or table in detail.

Narrative Flow

To summarize the Graphics Synchronization techniques, let's take all that you've learned in the last two chapters and put them into a high-level contextual view of your storyboard, as in Figure 12.3. This approach will help you give your presentation a continuous narrative flow.

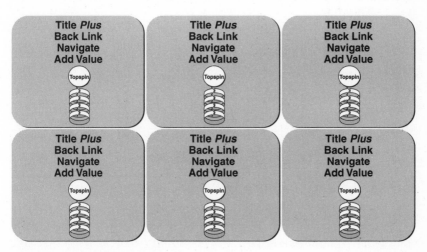

Figure 12.3 Narrative Flow

Start each inbound slide with a Title *Plus*, then Back Link to the outbound slide by using a word from its Title *Plus*. Use Verbal Navigation to explain the elements on the slide, then add value by citing supportive material that is *not* on the slide, and conclude with Topspin to either a Point B or a WIIFY, the powerful punctuating technique you read about in chapter 6. Continue on to treat each slide in the same manner.

Contrast this approach to the conventional "Now I'd like to . . ." followed by a straight verbatim reading of the slide. Instead, develop this fluid narrative rhythm. Combine your words, the Verbal, with your voice, the Vocal, and your body language, the Visual, as well as your graphics into an integrated whole. Make your presentation easy for your audience to follow, and your audiences will follow your lead.

The Trilogy: Inseparable and Disruptive

This concludes the exposition of the fundamental delivery skills techniques. You'll see their application in the concluding two chapters of *The Power Presenter* which, along with my two other books, *Presenting to Win* and *In the Line of Fire*, form the trilogy of the Power Presentations methodology.

There are two important culminating points about the methodology in all three books—as well as in every presentation or speech you will *ever* give. The first is that all the concepts must work together inseparably. Any one element can impact the others, as well as the fate of your entire presentation. To wit:

- You can develop a persuasive story and have it ruined by what is known as *Death by PowerPoint*.
- You can develop a persuasive story, illustrate it with dazzling graphics and have it ruined during your delivery by your own Fight-or-Flight Syndrome.

- You can develop a persuasive story, illustrate it with dazzling graphics, present it with poise and confidence, and have it ruined by a presentation environment that challenges and/or distracts your audience.
- You can develop a persuasive story, illustrate it with dazzling graphics, present it with poise and confidence in a presentation environment with all the trappings of a first-class, modern theater and have your audience listen to you in hushed awe for the full length of your presentation.
- But if, when you open the floor to questions, you react to the first tough question defensively, evasively, or contentiously, everything that went before will be negated.

Address every element thoroughly.

The second culminating point is that the Power Presentations approach to address each of the preceding mission-critical factors, when compared to established approaches, is disruptive. Today, presentations are conventionally done this way:

- Story/Graphics: Presentation stories are subordinated to a frantic scrambling together of PowerPoint slides, conflating two separate functions. This process results in slides that, in addition to their illustration function, also multitask as speaker prompts, leave behinds, and send aheads. The preparation process is treated in like manner: delegated to others and then relegated to rushed, last-minute run-throughs.
- Delivery Skills: Presenters and speakers, already driven by their adrenaline, are driven further to perform as cheerleaders or actors. To survive the stress, these anxious presenters turn their backs to their audiences during their presentations and read their slides verbatim.
- Presentation environments: Room arrangements, if addressed at all, are left to either the janitorial staff or the waiters.

- Q&A: Presenters are instructed to answer the questions they want to answer and not the ones that are asked.

Sound familiar?

In the next chapter, you'll find a compelling case study that illustrates how to, and how *not* to, address each of these essential elements effectively.

CHAPTER 13

The Power Presentations Pyramid

The scenarios at the end of the previous chapter contain five essential elements that exist in every presentation or speech, and can be viewed as the tiers of a pyramid, as in Figure 13.1.

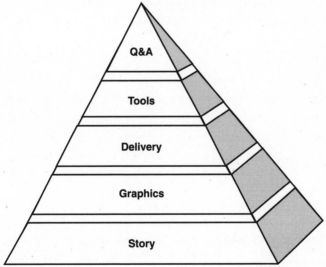

Figure 13.1   The Five Essential Elements of Every Presentation

The foundation of the pyramid, as it is for every presentation, is a solid story that is illustrated by the graphics of the slide show. In turn, these elements are delivered by the presenter's body language and voice, all supported by the tools of the presentation trade. The entire presentation is then subject to the scrutiny of the audience's questions, which the presenter must handle with complete assurance and credibility.

To demonstrate each of these five concepts, let's turn to an example that took place more than a decade and a half ago on the *Larry King Live* television program. In the November 9, 1993 episode, then-Vice President Al Gore debated Ross Perot about the proposed North American Free Trade Agreement (NAFTA). I analyzed this debate extensively in my book *In the Line of Fire* to demonstrate how *not* to answer questions as Perot did, a striking example of negative behavior.

Perot's behavior throughout the debate also serves to demonstrate how *not* to handle all the other elements of a presentation or a speech—the entire pyramid. Conversely, and more to the point, Al Gore's positive behavior in the same encounter serves to illustrate the correct way to manage each of those same essential elements.

The following sections of the debate illustrate each of the layers of the pyramid, starting at the foundation.

Note

To see all the video clips from the NAFTA debate with commentary, please visit www.powerltd.com/tpp and use the pass code you saw in the introduction. The sequence contains Video Frames 13.1 through 13.6.

Story

During his opening statement, Gore declared:

We said from the very beginning that we wanted to include the basic arrangement, which we did, with these side agreements.

"We," "we," "we": Gore began just as the U. S. Constitution begins: "We the people . . ." The inclusive pronoun *we* combines the self-centered *I* and the persuasive *you* into the mutually beneficial first-person plural. Gore was speaking about the Clinton administration but, by using the inclusive pronoun, he involved the electorate—and the audience. Audience Advocacy.

He continued:

And the reason why this is so important can be illustrated by the story of a good friend of mine that I grew up with, named Gordon Thompson . . .

Here Gore offered anecdotal evidence to support his cause. One of the most effective ways to communicate with any audience is to put your message in human-interest terms; it immediately evokes empathy.

. . . who lives in Elmwood, Tennessee, with his wife, Sue, and his son, Randy. He makes tires for a living. He's a member of the United Rubber Workers, and he's for this, because he's taken the time to look at how it affects his job and his family. We make the best tires in the world, but we have a hard time selling them in Mexico because they have a 20 percent tax collected at the border on all of the tires that we try to sell. Now when they make tires and sell them into the United States, the tax at the border is zero. So it's a one-way street. NAFTA changes that.

"NAFTA changes that," is a strong conclusion that reinforces Gore's position in support of NAFTA. This is Gore's key message, or his Point B—his Topspin.

Gore then seized the opportunity to Topspin again by giving the audience a reason to support NAFTA.

It makes it even-steven.

"It makes it even-steven" says that NAFTA is good for everybody. That's a benefit for the audience, or a WIIFY, the acronym for "What's In It For *You?*" Audience Advocacy again.

Gore's opening statement was inclusive, illustrative, beneficial, and, therefore, effective. Now let's look at Ross Perot's opening statement.

My concern is very simple. I look at many years experience in the maquilladora program . . .

"My concern" and "I look": For a man with a reputation of arrogance and egocentricity, *I*, the exclusive pronoun, served to reinforce his negative reputation. Note how many times he said "I" in his opening statement.

. . . and here is what I see. We have a lot of experience in Mexico. I've been accused of looking in the rearview mirror. That's right! I'm looking back at reality! And here is what I see after many years. Mexican workers' life—standard of living and pay has gone down, not up. After many years of having U.S. companies in Mexico, this is the way Mexican workers live all around a big, new U.S. plant.

At that point Perot held up a photograph of Tijuana, Mexico, and said:

Now just think if you owned a big U.S. company, and you went down to see the new U.S. plant, and you found slums all around it, your first reaction would be, "Why did you build a plant in the middle of slums?"

Perot concluded his opening remarks with a divisive, derogatory, and dismissive statement. No Audience Advocacy there.

Now let's move up the pyramid to illustrate the next major element.

Graphics

In a later segment of the debate, Gore held up a graphic card, the one shown in Video Frame 13.1. It contained one title, one subtitle, two dates, two numbers, and two bars: the gain bar in gold, the loss bar in red. The chart follows the simple formula: Less Is More. Less in the graphic is more effective. Less is easier for the audience to absorb. Less Is More is synonymous with Audience Advocacy.

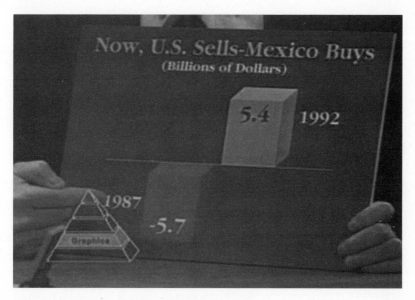

Video Frame 13.1   Al Gore's Graphic Card

Thirteen years after the NAFTA debate, Gore's affinity for effective graphics earned him an Academy Award. Throughout his career, and particularly during and after his vice-presidential terms, one of his principle concerns was about global warming. He developed a slide show on the subject that he delivered around the world many times over. In 2006, he made a film of the slide show, called *An Inconvenient Truth*. The film won an Oscar, the book version of the film became a bestseller, and the subject earned him a Nobel Prize in 2007. Not a bad haul for a subject that began life as a presentation.

In comparison, look at Perot's graphic, shown in Video Frame 13.2. Here we see the diametric opposite: More is less effective. More is clutter. Clutter makes the graphic difficult for the audience to absorb. Clutter forces the audience to try to interpret the graphic. When an audience's eyes are otherwise engaged, they stop listening to the speaker.

Video Frame 13.2   Ross Perot's Graphic Card

During Gore's discussion of his graphic, the television image cut to a wide shot that immediately highlighted the difference between the two men's physical expression of their message, as well as the next tier of the pyramid.

Body Language

In Video Frame 13.3, you see that Perot's head is tilted down. His facial features are in a scowl, his arms are in body wrap, and in the full motion video, his fingers are tapping impatiently on the desktop. He exhibits both Fight *and* Flight.

Video Frame 13.3   Body Language of Al Gore and Ross Perot

Gore, in direct contrast, is sitting up straight. His features are animated. He is making solid Eye *Connect* with Larry King. As Gore addressed King, he extended his arm with his palm open, as in a handshake; a perfect example of how Eye *Connect* and Reach out produce animation, or ERA. As Gore leaned forward, his chin dipped; and of course, when Gore's chin dipped, so did Larry King's. The television host represents the audience: When Larry King nods, the audience nods empathically.

A later section of the debate serves to illustrate another aspect of body language. In this sequence, Gore accused Perot of withholding information.

He does not want to publicly release how much money he's spending. How much money he's received from other sources to campaign against NAFTA.

Perot's reaction to Gore's accusation is seen in Video Frame 13.4. His hands and arms are in the defensive body wrap position. His left hand, (highlighted in the image) is tightly clenching two pens, as if he is preparing to use them as weapons—as if sending the silent message, "I'm gonna poke yo' eye out!"

Video Frame 13.4   Ross Perot Reacts to Al Gore's Accusation

Now let's move up to the penultimate layer of the pyramid, one of the subjects in chapter 12.

Tools of the Trade

Please refer back to Video Frame 13.3 and note that Gore's graphic card was positioned to his left, which is the favorable side because Western audiences read from left to right. Now look at Video Frame 13.5 to see that Perot's card is at his right, the unfavorable side because it forces the audience to read backward and across the grain.

Video Frame 13.5 Ross Perot's Graphic Card Positioned to His Right

The positions of these graphic cards were *not* accidental. The proof comes in the next section of the video, taken from the beginning of the program, when Larry King announced the ground rules.

To decide who got to sit where, we tossed a coin earlier today. The vice president won, and chose the inside seat.

The vice president chose the correct seat, making his graphic card, designed according to the Less Is More principle, even easier for the audience to read.

Now, we move forward in the debate to illustrate the top tier of the pyramid.

Q&A

In this segment of the debate, Perot again took up the attack against Mexico.

All right, folks, the Rio Grande River is the most polluted river in the Western Hemisphere . . .

Larry King asked:

But all of this is without NAFTA, right?

Gore interjected:

Yeah, and let me respond to this, if I could, would you . . .

Perot disregarded Gore.

Larry, Larry, this is after years of U.S. companies going to Mexico, living free . . .

Larry King responded:

But they could do that without NAFTA.

Perot answered Larry King:

But we can stop that without NAFTA and we can stop that with a good NAFTA.

Gore asked Perot:

How do you stop that without NAFTA?

Annoyed, Perot swung around to face Gore.

Just make . . . just cut that out. Pass a few simple laws on this, make it very, very clear . . .

Quite innocently, Gore asked Perot:

Pass a few simple laws on Mexico?

Perot shook his head, then dropped it like a bull about to charge, and said,

No.

Gore persisted, quietly, but firmly.

How do you stop it without NAFTA?

Perot snapped angrily:

Give me your whole mind.

"Give me your whole mind"! Perot addressed the vice president of the United States as if he were an office boy. In response, the vice president of the United States smiled back broadly.

The point here, and the point throughout *In the Line of Fire,* is that anger is *not* the way to respond to tough questions; equanimity is. This vital lesson applies to tough questions in *every* communication situation; not just in political debate, but also in business, public, social, and particularly—as anyone who has ever squabbled with his or her significant other can attest—interpersonal exchange.

With equanimity, Gore said to Perot:

Yeah, I'm listening. I haven't heard the answer, but go ahead.

Perot snapped again:

That's because you haven't quit talking.

Gore replied:

Well, I'm listening . . .

And for the third time, Gore calmly repeated his question:

How do you stop it without NAFTA?

Perot could not be calm. He snapped:

Okay, are you going to listen? Work on it![1]

"Work on it!" Another condescending crack of the whip.

The look on Gore's face in Video Frame 13.6 sums up his composed response to Perot's anger.

Video Frame 13.6   Al Gore's Reaction to Ross Perot's Anger

The impact of Ross Perot's negative behavior on audience perception was evident from the public opinion polls taken by *BusinessWeek* on the day before and the day after the debate, and shown here in Figure 13.2.[2]

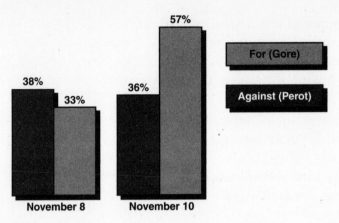

Figure 13.2　Public Opinion Polls on NAFTA, 1993

In the two days between the polls, the only factor or event with any impact on the NAFTA issue was that televised debate. Eleven million people watched *Larry King Live* that night, the highest rated cable program to that date (a distinction it held for 13 years until *Monday Night Football* moved from network broadcast to cable). Two months after the debate, Congress passed the NAFTA. Clearly, Ross Perot's negative behavior swung the undecided respondents against his position.

The NAFTA debate provides us with a summary of all the major elements in this book. A Power Presentation can be viewed as an operating system. Just as Microsoft Windows controls multiple software applications, the Power Presentations pyramid controls and integrates all the essential communication dynamics:

- *Story.* Organize your content so that it is relevant, focused, and has a logical flow. Every story must have a clear objective, stated as a call to action, or Point B, and a benefit, stated as a WIIFY, if not multiple WIIFYs. Once you have developed your story, Verbalize it extensively.
- *Graphics.* You are the focus of your presentation; your graphics are there *only* to support you. Design all your graphics in adherence to the Less Is More principle, and introduce those graphics with

animation that helps illustrate your story. Be aware of how your audiences perceive your images with their conditioned responses (in Western culture, text reads from left to right) and their neurological responses (the human eye reacts reflexively to new images).

- *Delivery skills.* What you say is impacted by how you say it and what you do when you say it. Deliver your story to one person at a time in phrases that Complete the Arc and are accompanied by Eye Connect and Reach out; all of which combine to produce Animation. Speak *Only* to Eyes. Use the *Mental Method of Presenting* to interact with your audience by Reading their Reactions and being prepared to Adjust your Content.

- *Tools of the trade.* Position yourself and your tools so that your audience can easily see you and your graphics. Make it easy for your audience and they will make it easy for you.

- *Pause.* All these dynamic elements orbit around a central unifying nucleus, shown in Figure 13.3.

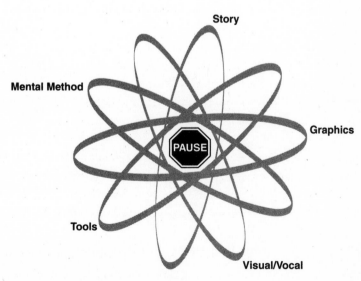

Figure 13.3   The Power Presentation

The ultimate conclusion is that a presentation does not exist on the screen alone, in the presenter alone, or in the audience alone. A Power Presentation combines all these dynamic elements into a living entity that changes every time you present.

CHAPTER 14

Coda—Ending with the Beginning

Behavior that's admired is the path to power among people everywhere.

—*Beowulf*, Seomus Heaney, translator[1]

The First Day on the Job

Upon graduation from Stanford University with my master of arts degree in speech, drama, and television, I was hired as an associate adjunct professor of speech (translation: teaching assistant) at the Baruch School of the College of the City of New York. My first assignment was to teach the requisite beginners' course in public speaking. On the first day, in the first class, the first question asked of me was the one that was to become the most frequently asked throughout my career as a presentations coach. At the start of the class, an extremely nervous young woman came up to me and implored, "What do I do with my hands?"

Hands weren't part of the curriculum at Stanford. My graduate studies had included Aristotle, Socrates, and Cicero, but not gestures. "Uh, oh!" I said to myself, "I can't look stupid on my first day on the job!"

As I frantically searched the database of my mind for an answer, my adrenaline-driven eyes frantically searched the classroom for an escape route. Suddenly, they stopped at the pen on my desk. "An orator is a scholar," I said, feigning assured wisdom. "Use a scholar's tool; use a pen. Hold onto your pen to focus your energies. That's a logical place for your hands."

My improvised remedy seemed to produce an immediate cure for the young woman's jitters. Confident that I had made a major discovery that would become a landmark in the annals of rhetoric, and that I would be hailed as a twentieth-century Aristotle, I continued to prescribe the remedy to other students for the next two semesters. In support of my advice, I role-modeled the solution by holding onto my own pen as I lectured. I was not only telling people what to do, I was doing it myself. Behavioral psychologists call this *double reinforcement*.

A year later, I developed a new module for the speech class and dutifully went home to practice it in front of a mirror. What I saw made me realize that my brilliant new solution had created the image of a person who was brandishing a weapon, making a fist, and protecting his underbelly, all at the same time. I had been repeating this negative behavior for a year and reinforcing it by advocating it, until it became a deeply ingrained habit. I knew I had to break it, and the effort was like trying to rip adhesive tape off my skin. But I did it. I learned to eliminate the body wrap and to Reach out. You, too, can learn to Reach out. You, too, can change your behavior and achieve positive new results in front of your audiences.

Bookends

The first exemplary speaker in this book was Ronald Reagan, the Great Communicator. His superior qualities merit a reprise here to serve as a lasting role model for you and for any other person who aspires to stand in front of any audience and win them over. Reagan's eight-year stint as the host of *General Electric Theater* was the seed from which his rich repertory of skills blossomed. It is also the same seed possessed by every human being who converses with another human being.

You, and 99 percent of the presenters and speakers I have ever encountered, are not actors or performers. If you treat your Moments of Truth in front of your mission-critical audiences as performances, you are sure to fail. If, instead, you treat those vital moments as individual conversations, you are defaulting to what you do naturally and effectively.

That shift in your approach, along with a shift in your thinking from yourself to the person with whom you are conversing, is the essence of the Mental Method of Presenting. These shifts will evoke empathy from your audiences *involuntarily*. In turn, when you perceive their positive responses, your fear of public speaking will glide easily into a comfort zone, like a billowing parachute lifted by the wind.

Joe Moglia, whom you met in chapter 7, merits a reprise for his perceptions about the learning process. As Joe put it, "The key to effectuating change is . . . that the discomfort is the price you pay to achieve new results."

The price you will pay to achieve your new results is certain to produce discomfort in two areas:

- The pause.
- Reach out.

I certainly experienced discomfort in each of these areas, by nurture and nature. As a native of New York, I was nurtured to believe that pausing is worse than capitulating; as a human being, my nature was to assume the fetal position with my hands and arms. But I changed. I changed because I understood the power of interpersonal communication, and the importance of doing well at it. You can change, too.

The Best Compliment

In the previous chapter, I indicated that all the concepts in the pyramid apply to every presentation or speech you will ever give. Let me extend that observation here for a moment of immodesty, if I may. Allow me to share with you the best compliment I ever received in my two decades as a presentations coach. It came from Cindy Burgdorf, the former CFO of SanDisk Corporation, now the world's largest supplier of flash memory data storage products. In 1995, Cindy and Eli Harari, the CEO and founder of the company, had just concluded the preparations for their IPO road show with the last of four intensive days of the Power Presentations program. As we were wrapping up, Cindy turned to me and said, "This isn't just about presentations is it? This is about communicating in any situation. It all applies everywhere."

I hope Cindy's words are meaningful to you, too. *Every* communication exchange you make—whether in a meeting, an interview, a conference, a discussion, or a one-on-one engagement; whether business or social or political—involves the same key elements and dynamics that are in a presentation or speech. They vary only slightly, and only by degree. If you want your communication to be successful, you must manage all the elements and dynamics of every interpersonal exchange effectively. If you want a positive audience perception, you must present with positive behavior.

Behavior that's admired is the path to power among people everywhere.

Good luck.

ACKNOWLEDGMENTS

Benji Rosen, my Stanford University graduate school buddy, who studied electrical engineering while I was learning about Aristotle and Aeschylus in the Department of Speech and Drama. Nearly thirty years later, Ben saw the opportunity to merge the two disciplines in the fertile garden that had sprouted in Stanford's backyard, Silicon Valley. It was Ben's inspiration and impetus that gave rise to Power Presentations, Ltd. and to the two decades of client programs that gave rise to the disruptive methodology in this book.

One of Ben's first introductions was to Bill Davidow, who championed not only the inception of the methodology but also its culmination as a book by introducing me to James Levine of the Levine-Greenberg Literary Agency. Jim resoundingly disproves Fred Allen's classic description of agents, "All the sincerity in Hollywood you can stuff into a flea's navel and still have room left over to conceal eight caraway seeds and an agent's heart." Jim, with the able assistance of Lindsay Edgecombe, Beth Fisher, and Kerry Evans, extended Bill's synergy by introducing me to Richard Narramore, my editor at John Wiley and Sons, Inc.

Richard, ably supported by Tiffany Groglio, Ann Kenny, Lauren Freestone, and Janice Borzendowski, brought fresh insight to material that took two decades to evolve.

James Christopher Welch is the rod and Nichole Nears is the staff that comfort and support me in the considerable task of operating Power Presentations. Each of them has also been there every step along the way in the creation of this book: Father Jim with his wise business acumen and powerful personal values; Nichole with her dazzling graphics, resonant feedback, paranormal legal acuity, and diligent manuscript and source control. Jennifer Turcotte, who has moved on and yet stayed with us, provided superior background research and archival video management when I started the manuscript. Pearl Cheung has succeeded Jennifer admirably, hardly skipping a beat (except at mealtime). Nichole was preceded by Susan Hill, Jennifer Haydon, and Nancy Price, all of whom contributed to supporting the program. Rich Hall, the quiet man behind the digital video camera and in the control room, speaks volumes behind the scenes with his mirror neurons. Sixtus Oeschle, the latest addition to the company, arrived in time to contribute his technical, rhetorical, and video skills, along with a shared appreciation of Dizzy Gillespie.

Bill Immerman left his law practice to immerse himself in a successful film production career, but kept me as his only private client and, in doing so, was there to provide the valuable legal counsel that this book required.

Kenn Rabin of Fulcrum Media Services went to the ends of the earth to find and, in some cases, unearth, the many video and film clip examples that support my concepts. Kenn worked closely with Brian Fulford, the Senior Licensing Agent of CNN, who provided the bulk of the source videos. Those videos were edited by Ed Rudolph and Bob Johns, the artists-in-residence at Video Arts, San Francisco, a superb production house managed by Kim Salyer and David Weissman. David is no relative, but I wish he were.

Bill Salisbury of Morgan Stanley and George Lee of Goldman Sachs, my constant supporters in the IPO arena, gave me deep perspective into that most critical of mission-critical presentations, the road show.

Joe Bellanoff, MD, James H. Sabry, MD, Herbert Dedo, MD, Krzysztof Izdebski, PhD, and particularly Frank Perlroth, MD—who gave me scientific validation, and gives me good health and many laughs.

Melvin Van Peebles showed me the difference between critics and performers, and therefore between talk and action.

Thanks to the hundreds of people at Cisco Systems and Microsoft who learned, practiced, and then went on to champion the Power Presentations method. Among the Cisco Kids are: Peter Alexander, Joe Ammirato (now of Woven Systems), Lina Arseneault, Sue Bostrom, Toby Burton, Heather Gallegos, Mary Gorges, John Growdon, Lauren Hasenhuttl, Marie Hattar, Sharon Hume, Seema Kumar, Inbar Lasser-Raab, Hardy Lipscomb, Corinne Marsolier, Christophe Metivier, Mohsen Moazami, Istvan Papp (now of Magyar Telekom), Rajiv Ramaswami, Jennifer Robinson-McAdams, Linda Sergides, and my favorite dinner partner, Kaan Terzigolou. Among the Microsofties are: Orlando Ayala, Aziz Ben Malek, Raj Biyani, Ilya Buhkshteyn, Kimberly Kay Butler, Mark Croft, Will Flash, Debbie Fry-Wilson, Linda Heffernan, Lynn Hill, Kimberly Ishoy, Sarah Jamieson, Ted Kummert, Arun Lal, Andy Lees, Pascal Martin, Vince Mendillo, Dave Mendlen, Mike Nash, Doreen Parker, Shira Sagiv, Paul Sausville, Dave Thompson, Chris Vandenberg, Sarah Williams, Lori Woehler, and Simon Witts. Jim LeValley championed the techniques at both Cisco and Microsoft.

Two of the Microsoft alumni, both named Jon, merit special mention. Jon Bromberg, the Max Bialystock of the Big Tent and the (not-so) Little Screen kept his (often) steady hand on the zoom from digital stills to High-8 to Digital Beta tape to DVD to YouTube to streaming video. The other Jon, Lazarus, a former New York television producer who moved to Seattle to work for Microsoft, invited me to work with Microsoft executives in 1989, an assignment I continue to fill this day. But I am particularly grateful to this Jon who, while accepting of my techniques in that early session, challenged the difficulty of the learning process. Jon's challenge gave rise to the Comfort Zone Paradox: "What feels comfortable looks uncomfortable; what feels uncomfortable looks comfortable."

I am also grateful to the people who granted me permission to discuss my work with them: Will Poole, Olivier Fontana, and Marya

McCabe of Microsoft; Jeff Raikes, formerly with Microsoft, and now with the Bill and Melinda Gates Foundation; Steve Goldman of Isilon Systems; Joe Moglia of TD Ameritrade; Lawrence Steinman, MD, of Bayhill Therapeutics and Stanford University; Leslie Culbertson of Intel; Katherine Crothall of Animas; Eric Tardif now of Morgan Stanley; and Cindy Burgdorf formerly of SanDisk Corporation.

And for their individual contributions: Don Valentine, the man with THE quote; Warren Drabek of Express Permissions, who did all the work I had to do when I wrote my Master's thesis; and David Woodward of the Stanford Graduate School of Business who defined the full length of the presentation field.

My kids, Bixby, the resounding sounding board, and Natalie, the Aggressive Reader Extraordinaire, who earned a well-deserved place next to Roberta Baron, the PitA Extraordinaire, and to Lydia Liberman, the literary lioness.

My Lovely Lady Lucie for the Pyongyang point as well as all the other points of the compass in the universe . . . and her unconditional love.

NOTES

Introduction

1. Kathleen Pender, "Prep School for High-Tech Execs: Coach Specializes in IPO Road Shows," *San Francisco Chronicle*, July 9, 1990.
2. Tom McNichol, "How to Go Public," *Business 2.0*, July 2007.
3. John Lahr, "Petrified: The Horrors of Stagefright," *New Yorker*, August 28, 2006.

Chapter 1

1. A. Mehrabian, *Silent Messages: Implicit Communication of Emotions and Attitudes* (Belmont, CA: Wadsworth, 1981).
2. Transcript, August 15, 1988 courtesy CNN.
3. Howard Rosenberg, "Ronald Reagan's Farewell: The Power and the Glory," *Los Angeles Times*, August 16, 1988.
4. Oliver Sacks, *The Man Who Mistook His Wife for a Hat and Other Clinical Tales* (New York, NY: Touchstone, 2002).
5. Warren Hoge, "A Speech That Khrushchev or Arafat or Che Would Admire," *New York Times*, September 24, 2006.
6. http://en.wikipedia.org/?title=Marcel_Marceau; accessed October 7, 2008.
7. David McNeill, Justine Cassell, and Karl-Erik McCullough, "Communicative Effects of Speech-Mismatched Gestures," in *Research on Language & Social Interaction*, Vol. 27, No. 3, 1994: 223.

Chapter 2

1. Daniel Goleman, *Social Intelligence: The New Science of Human Relationships* (New York: Bantam, 2006).
2. Tania Singer, Ben Seymour, John O'Doherty, Holger Kaube, Raymond J. Dolan, and Chris D. Frith, "Empathy for Pain Involves the Affective But Not Sensory Components of Pain," *Science*, Vol. 303, No. 20, February 2004.
3. G. di Pellegrino, L. Fadiga, L. Fogassi, V. Gallese, and G. Rizzolatti, "Understanding Motor Events: A Neurophysiological Study," *Experimental Brain Research*, Vol. 91, No. 1, October, 1992: 176–180.
4. Transcript of Bob Dole's speech, May 15, 1996, courtesy CNN.
5. 1996 Poll source: http://edition.cnn.com/ALLPOLITICS/1996/news/9605/13/poll.issues/poll.shtml.orig.
6. Transcript of Barack Obama's speech, July 27, 2004, courtesy CNN.
7. Elissa Gootman, Patrick Healy, Micheal Janofsky, Michael Luo, Jennifer Medina, Robert Pear, Richard Prez-Pea, Marc Santora, Stephanie Strom, and Daniel J. Wakin, "The 2004 Elections: State by State—Midwest; Some Important Victories for Kerry, But a Death Blow in Ohio," *New York Times*, November 4, 2004.

Chapter 4

1. "Workspaces: A Look at Where People Work," *Wall Street Journal*, January 30, 2002.

Chapter 5

1. Transcript of George W. Bush's speech, "Subliminable," September 12, 2000, courtesy ABC News Video Source.
2. Transcript of George W. Bush's Inaugural Address, January 20, 2001 courtesy CNN.
3. Bill Clinton, *My Life* (New York: Random House, Inc., 2004).
4. R. W. Apple Jr., "The Democrats in Atlanta; Dukakis's Speech Offers His 'Vision of America'," New York Times, July 22, 1988.
5. Bill Clinton, op. cit.

6. Bill Clinton, op. cit.
7. Transcript of Clinton farewell address, August 14, 2000, courtesy CNN.
8. Devlin Barrett, "Bill Clinton's Speech Income Shrinks," Associated Press, accessed June 14, 2004, www.accessmylibrary.com/coms2/summary_0286-21638256_ITM.
9. Mike McIntire, "Clintons Made $109 Million in Last 8 Years," *New York Times*, April 5, 2008.

Chapter 6

1. Russell Adams, "Getting Your Head in the Game: From the World Cup to Youth Tennis, a Training Fad Emerges; the Science of Finding the Zone," *Wall Street Journal*, July 29, 2006.
2. Timothy Gallwey, *The Inner Game of Tennis*, (New York: Random House, 1974).
3. Adam Nagourney, Marjorie Connelly, and Dahlia Sussman, "Polls Find Voters Weighing Issues vs. Electability," *New York Times*, November 14, 2007.
4. Ryan Lizza, "The Relaunch: Can Barack Obama Catch Hillary Clinton?" *New Yorker*, November 26, 2007.
5. "Iowa's Caucuses Results," *New York Times*, January 8, 2008.
6. "Barack Obama's Caucus Speech and Hillary Clinton's Caucus Speech," *New York Times*, January 3, 2008.
7. Karl Rove, "Why Hillary Won," *Wall Street Journal*, January 10, 2008.
8. www.barackobama.com, accessed October 10, 2008.
9. Transcript of Libby Dole's speech, August 14, 1996, courtesy CNN.
10. John Lahr, "Petrified: The Horrors of Stagefright," *New Yorker*, August 28, 2006.

Chapter 7

1. Marshall H. Klaus, John H. Kennell, and Phyllis Klaus, *Bonding: Building the Foundations of Secure Attachment and Independence* (New York, NY: Da Capo, 1996).

2. Transcript of Norman Schwarzkopf's speech, courtesy CNN.

3. Transcript of Kennedy/Nixon debate, September 26, 1960, courtesy, John F. Kennedy Library.

4. Copyright © 2006, the Gallup Organization. All rights reserved. Reprinted with permission from www.gallup.com.

5. Richard Milhous Nixon, *Six Crises* (New York: Doubleday, 1969).

6. Don Hewitt, *Tell Me a Story: Fifty Years and 60 Minutes in Television* (New York, NY: Public Affairs, 2002).

Chapter 8

1. Nat Hentoff, "She's on the Road to Renown," By Nat Hentoff, *Wall Street Journal*, September 5, 2007.

2. Claude Steinberg, "Dazed and Confused: Possible Processing Constraints on Emotional Response to Information-Dense Motivational Speech," in from *Emotions in the Human Voice*, Volume III, Krzysztof Izdebski, PhD, ed. (San Diego, CA: Plural Publishing, 2007).

3. Kate Julian, "When in Pyongyang," *New Yorker*, March 3, 2008.

4. Transcript of George W. Bush and Al Gore, final debate, October 17, 2000. www.debates.org/pages/trans2000c.html; accessed October 7, 2008.

5. Transcript of George W. Bush speech, September 20, 2001, www.whitehouse.gov/news/releases/2001/09/20010920-8.html; accessed October 7, 2008.

6. Transcript of George W. Bush and Vladimir Putin press conference, November 13, 2001, www.whitehouse.gov/news/releases/2001/11/20011114-1.html; accessed October 7, 2008.

7. Transcript of George W. Bush's January 28, 2008 State of the Union address, www.whitehouse.gov/stateoftheunion/2008/index.html; accessed October 7, 2008.

Chapter 9

1. Transcript of Ronald Reagan's January 25, 1988 State of the Union address, 1988, www.thisnation.com/library/sotu/1988rr.html; accessed October 7, 2008.

2. Transcript of Winston Churchill's December 26, 1941 address to the joint session of Congress, http://www.winstonchurchill.org/files/public/FinestHour129.pdf, accessed November 10, 2008.

3. http://www.americanrhetoric.com/speeches/jfkinaugural.htm, accessed November 10, 2008.

4. License granted by Intellectual Properties Management, Atlanta, Georgia, manager of the King estate.

5. The *Time* 100: The Most Important People of the Century, Heroes & Icons, www.time.com/time/time100/heroes/profile/graham02.html; accessed October 7, 2008.

6. Reverend Billy Graham, courtesy *NBC News* Archives.

7. Transcript of *General Electric Theater*, November 14, 1954, courtesy Ronald Reagan Presidential Library.

8. Alec MacGillis, "Finding Political Strength in the Power of Words," *Washington Post*, February 26, 2008.

9. Barack Obama, *The Audacity of Hope* (New York: Crown, 2006).

10. George Will, "Why Obama Should Take the Leap," *Wall Street Journal*, February 14, 2006.

Chapter 10

1. Quoted in William Finnegan, "The Candidate," *New Yorker*, May 31, 2004.

2. www.tnr.com/politics/story.html?id=aaad0724-dd13-4ffa-810b-d5d3220ff055, accessed October 10, 2008.

3. Monica Davey, "The 2004 Campaign: The Illinois Primary; from Crowed Field, Democrats Choose State Legislator to Seek Senate Seat," *New York Times*, March 17, 2004.

4. Finnegan, *op.cit.*

5. http://www.hillaryclinton.com/news/release/view/?id=6467, accessed October 10, 2008.

6. Alec MacGillis, "Finding Political Strength in the Power of Words," *Washington Post*, February 26, 2008.

7. www.realclearpolitics.com/epolls/2008/president/us/democratic_presidential_nomination-191.html, accessed October 10, 2008.

8. MacGillis, *op. cit.*

9. MacGillis, *op. cit.*

10. Finnegan, *op. cit.*
11. http://www.americanrhetoric.com/speeches/gettysburgaddress.htm, accessed November 10, 2008.
12. http://www.americanrhetoric.com/speeches/jfkinaugural.htm, accessed November 10, 2008.
13. Transcript of Barack Obama's speech, July 27, 2004, courtesy of CNN.
14. http://www.americanrhetoric.com/speeches/jfkinaugural.htm, accessed November 10, 2008.
15. Obama, *op. cit.*
16. http://www.cnn.com/2008/POLITICS/11/04/Obama.transcript/index.html, accessed November 7, 2008.
17. Winston Churchill, courtesy ABC News Video Source.
18. Obama, *op. cit.*
19. Presidential debate transcript, courtesy of CNN.
20. Michael Duffy and Nancy Gibbs, "Can Obama Play Offense?" *Time*, March 6, 2008.
21. MacGillis, *op. cit.*
22. www.youtube.com/watch?v=zrp-v2tHaDo accessed, October 10, 2008.
23. Peggy Noonan, "A Thinking Man's Speech," *Wall Street Journal*, March 21, 2008.
24. http://www.cnn.com/2008/POLITICS/08/29/rollins.palin/index.html

Chapter 13

1. *Larry King Live*, CNN.
2. *BusinessWeek*, November 22, 1993.

Chapter 14

1. Seamus Heaney, *Beowulf: A New Verse Translation* (New York: W.W. Norton, 2000).

INDEX